T0001922

## THAT'S THE WAY OF

### Praise for the series:

It was only a matter of time before a clever publisher realized that there is an audience for whom *Exile on Main Street* or *Electric Ladyland* are as significant and worthy of study as *The Catcher in the Rye* or *Middlemarch* . . . The series . . . is freewheeling and eclectic, ranging from minute rock-geek analysis to idiosyncratic personal celebration—*The New York Times Book Review*

Ideal for the rock geek who thinks liner notes just aren't enough—*Rolling Stone*

One of the coolest publishing imprints on the planet—*Bookslut*

These are for the insane collectors out there who appreciate fantastic design, well-executed thinking, and things that make your house look cool. Each volume in this series takes a seminal album and breaks it down in startling minutiae. We love these. We are huge nerds—*Vice*

A brilliant series . . . each one a work of real love—*NME* (UK)

Passionate, obsessive, and smart—*Nylon*

Religious tracts for the rock 'n' roll faithful—*Boldtype*

[A] consistently excellent series—*Uncut* (UK)

We . . . aren't naive enough to think that we're your only source for reading about music (but if we had our way . . . watch out). For those of you who really like to know everything there is to know about an album, you'd do well to check out Bloomsbury's "33 1/3" series of books— *Pitchfork*

For almost 20 years, the 33-and-a-Third series of music books has focused on individual albums by acts well known (Bob Dylan, Nirvana, Abba, Radiohead), cultish (Neutral Milk Hotel, Throbbing Gristle, Wire) and many levels in-between. The range of music and their creators defines "eclectic." while the writing veers from freewheeling to acutely insightful. In essence, the books are for the music fan who (as Rolling Stone noted) "thinks liner notes just aren't enough." —*The Irish Times*

**For reviews of individual titles in the series, please visit our blog at 333sound .com and our website at http://www.bloomsbury.com/musicandsoundstudies**

**Follow us on Twitter: @333books**

**Like us on Facebook: https://www.facebook.com/33.3books**

For a complete list of books in this series, see the back of this book.

Forthcoming in the series:

and many more . . .

# That's the Way of the World

## Dwight E. Brooks

BLOOMSBURY ACADEMIC
NEW YORK • LONDON • OXFORD • NEW DELHI • SYDNEY

BLOOMSBURY ACADEMIC
Bloomsbury Publishing Inc
1385 Broadway, New York, NY 10018, USA
50 Bedford Square, London, WC1B 3DP, UK
29 Earlsfort Terrace, Dublin 2, Ireland

BLOOMSBURY, BLOOMSBURY ACADEMIC and the Diana logo are trademarks of
Bloomsbury Publishing Plc

First published in the United States of America 2023

Copyright © Dwight E. Brooks, 2023

Library of Congress Cataloging-in-Publication Data

Names: Brooks, Dwight E. (Dwight Ernest) author.
Title: That's the way of the world / Dwight E. Brooks.
Description: [1st.] | New York, NY : Bloomsbury Academic, 2022. | Includes
bibliographical references and index. | Summary: "An analysis of EWF's world musical
artistry and their embodiment of innovative fusion of musical genres and homage to
African and American traditions"– Provided by publisher.
Identifiers: LCCN 2022015200 (print) | LCCN 2022015201 (ebook) | ISBN 9781501378058
(paperback) | ISBN 9781501378065 (epub) | ISBN 9781501378072 (pdf) | ISBN
9781501378089
Subjects: LCSH: Earth, Wind & Fire (Musical group). That's the way of the world. |
Soul music–History and criticism. | Funk (Music)–History and criticism. | Rhythm and
blues music–History and criticism. | Popular music–United States–1971-1980–History
and criticism.
Classification: LCC ML421.E185 B76 2022 (print) | LCC ML421.E185 (ebook) | DDC
782.42164092/2–dc23/eng/20220331
LC record available at https://lccn.loc.gov/2022015200
LC ebook record available at https://lccn.loc.gov/2022015201

ISBN: PB: 978-1-5013-7805-8
ePDF: 978-1-5013-7807-2
eBook: 978-1-5013-7806-5

Series: 33 ⅓

Typeset by Deanta Global Publishing Services, Chennai, India
Printed and bound in the United Kingdom

To find out more about our authors and books visit www.bloomsbury.com and sign up for
our newsletters.

# Contents

# Acknowledgments

I am grateful to Leah Babb-Rosenfeld, Rachel Moore, and their team at Bloomsbury for their editorial assistance and support. I am truly honored to work with Professor Samantha ("Sam") Bennett on the final drafts. She provided invaluable comments and insights that helped me achieve my vision for this book. This project would have never seen the light without the extensive insights from my "best man," Dr. William C. Banfield. Bill, recognized by Cornel West as a true Renaissance man, has been my "lil' bro" since we met at Indiana University, Bloomington, in the early 1990s. His music from IU's Soul Revue, our radio collaboration on "Landscapes in Color," and our trips to Cuba are among the many moments in which he broadened my love of music. I can only hope my love for him and his queen Krystal and support of his multidimensional creativity are sufficient expressions of gratitude for his willingness to embrace me as a nonmusician. I am especially indebted to my colleague and friend Loren Mulraine for his invaluable comments on my draft.

My greatest source of inspiration comes from Marie, the love of my life. Her unconditional support and belief in me allowed a two-year process to be a true labor of love. A jazz vocalist herself, Marie shared my daily Earth, Wind & Fire playlists—at home, in the car, from Nashville to New York, to Florida, and even in the United Arab Emirates. Her family of musicians made too many contributions to detail here. My "neph," D-Mile, one of the most talented producers in the contemporary music scene—and his father, Dernst, took the time from their busy professional music schedules to talk with me about this book. In fact, Dernst, the consummate teacher, may be one of the few whose admiration of Maurice White rivals my own. I have too many supportive colleagues to recognize here, but I must acknowledge Park Beede, Zoe Hurley, Ganga Dhanesh, and Andrea Juhasz—my "work wife"—for their collegiality and support. This book is inspired by many fond memories of dear friends such as Craig "Sack" Carter, Derrick Morris, and Asenath (Shipp) Wilburn, whose mutual love of Earth, Wind & Fire was evident at the EWF concerts we attended together. Much love to my daughter Dione who understood at a very early age my passion for Earth, Wind & Fire. Thanks to my brother Terry for introducing me to "Last Days and Time" and my parents for allowing me to go to North Philly's Uptown to see EWF fifty years ago.

My deepest appreciation goes to Verdine White for "Zooming" with me for more than two hours and recognizing my ear for music (I have the video to prove it). Verdine, the most down-to-earth brother I have ever met, provided a plethora of unforgettable moments of his experiences with EWF, alongside his thoughts on the Versus with the Isley Brothers and other topics. I also offer sincere thanks to Rich

Salvato for arranging the interview. Finally, the ultimate "thank you" goes to Maurice White. His concept and collaborative vision with Phillip Bailey, Ralph Johnson, Larry Dunn, the late Andrew Woolfolk, and the other members of Earth, Wind & Fire provide eternal dances for the world. I hope this little book does justice to their large musical legacy.

# Foreword

I am listening to *That's the Way of the World* as I reflect upon Dwight Brooks' writing about Earth, Wind & Fire. As an artist, composer, and educator, I developed a greater cultural appreciation for EWF after reading Brooks' contextual analysis. His commitment to great music matches the intentionality of EWF allowing readers to map the meanings in this great album. Every musical stroke of the musicians is linked to cultural values contained in the musical arrangements, lyrics, vocals, and performance. Brooks impeccably captures these values as well as music affectation, emotional, and cultural meanings. How we feel about this music further invites us to connect to shared values, "being soulfilled." Brooks brings music performance, history, and cultural impact together in ways that help us understand the worth of this exceptional recording.

Brooks' insightful and enthusiastic analysis allows us to join his journey into Earth, Wind & Fire's ascension to popular music royalty that was marked by *That's the Way of the World*. Brooks reminds us how songs tell the stories of life and become powerful vehicles for cultural ideas and personal reflection. His intellectual and artistic testimonies enhance our understanding of our places in the world and for that we are grateful.

William Banfield, musician

*Dr. William C. Banfield is a musician, composer, educator, and author. He served as Professor and Director of Africana Studies Center, Berklee College of Music, until his retirement in 2020. Cornel West called him "one of the last great Renaissance men in our time, a towering artist, exemplary educator, rigorous scholar, and courageous freedom fighter." Henry Louis Gates wrote that Banfield is "one of the most original voices on the scene today."*

# *Prologue*: That World Today

Music expresses that which cannot be put into words
and that which cannot remain silent.

*Victor Hugo*

*That's the Way of the World* (*TTWOTW*) was Earth, Wind &
Fire's (EWF) sixth studio album (1975) and reached number
one on both the *Billboard* 200 and Top Soul Albums charts.
It was certified as Triple Platinum in the United States by the
Recording Industry Association of America (RIAA). The
album generated EWF's first crossover hit, "Shining Star,"
which ascended to number one on both the *Billboard* Hot
100 and Hot Soul Singles charts. "Shining Star" also won
a Grammy Award for Best R&B Performance by a Duo or
Group with Vocals.

   *TTWOTW* was conceived initially as a soundtrack to a
film on corruption in the record industry. White ignored
the screenplay and abandoned traditional approaches to
recording a film score with one notable exception: At the
insistence of co-producer Charles Stepney, *TTWOTW*
included full orchestrations on several songs. Although

the film tanked, the album soared with eight songs that transcended musical genres in a unique blend of soul, blues, jazz, gospel, and funk. *TTWOTW* embodied many of the components that defined EWF's signature sound of message music delivered through layered vocals, accented by pulsating rhythms, powerful horns, musical interludes, and African-inspired cadences. The songs represented many of the shared experiences of the band members that resonated with listeners. *Rolling Stone*'s poll of artists, producers, critics, and music industry data ranked *TTWOTW* #420 on its list of the greatest albums of all time.[1]

I use the term "landmark" to characterize *TTWOTW*'s broader cultural and musical significance. The album propelled EWF onto a global stage it would not relinquish for the remainder of the decade. Following the success of *TTWOTW*, EWF's spectrum music spawned eight Platinum albums, six Grammys, four American Music Awards, inclusion on the Hollywood Walk of Fame, induction into the Rock and Roll Hall of Fame, and in 2019 into the Kennedy Center Honors.

Drummer, songwriter, music journalist, and film director Ahmir Khalib Thompson, known professionally as Questlove, offered a pitch-perfect Instagram post on the 2016 passing of Maurice White, the founder of EWF: "You know how hard it is to present Afrocentric jazz and spiritual positivity in the face of what we had to deal with in the 70s?".[2]

My central purpose is to provide a contextual analysis of *TTWOTW*. One important context of the album is the sociocultural historical moment surrounding EWF's evolution from 1970 to 1975. Black protest in the 1960s yielded modest political and economic gains in Black America. By the 1970s, Blacks began to embrace their own cultural traditions and establish new ways of seeing, representing, and expressing themselves. A second context to understand *TTWOTW* is the creative milieu of EWF's evolution during the early 1970s. Maurice White developed a concept for EWF that evolved into a collaborative musical vision that fused various styles of music in the service of humanity. A third context to understand *TTWOTW*'s prominence is through some of the broader changes in the music industry in the 1960s and 1970s, particularly as they impacted Black industry executives and Black music. *TTWOTW* not only shattered musical barriers but also paved the way for greater numbers of African American executives in the music industry.

Verdine White, an original member of EWF, told me *TTWOTW* was a "breakthrough" for the band. He described the album as "beautiful" and totally different from anything that he had ever heard or participated in.[3] Verdine beamed with pride telling me the album broke through many barriers. The cultural history of *TTWOTW* begins several years before 1975 and starts with Verdine's older brother Maurice White.

Maurice White was a 26-year-old drummer for The Ramsey Lewis Trio during what has been called the "long hot summer" of 1967. Black Americans engaged in civil disorder over institutional racism, lack of economic opportunities, political disenfranchisement, and police brutality. Widespread protests of the Vietnam War by many White Americans produced an unprecedented militarized policing on college campuses and cities with large Black populations. In 1967, Dr. Martin Luther King, Jr., branded riots in American cities as "the language of the unheard."[4] The federal government's response was highlighted by Richard Nixon's "law and order" presidential campaign and subsequent election in 1968.

The period from 1968 to 1972 perpetrated the twentieth century's most extensive state-sanctioned repression against Black Americans. The southern-based Civil Rights Movement and its nonviolent protest focus on desegregation were met with violent attacks on Black institutions such as schools and churches. The assassination of Dr. King was a major catalyst of the heightened volatility that expanded Black protest to include agency and autonomy in the forms of Black pride and power. As America's language of the unheard spread to popular music, one of the brashest Black voices was James Brown.

James Brown's 1968 hit "Say It Loud, I'm Black and I'm Proud" functioned in many of the same ways that music has always operated in the Black public sphere. As Mark Anthony Neal's brilliant analysis of the Black popular music tradition reveals, Black music functions primarily as a catalyst for creating and maintaining communities, including communal critiques of Black experiences.[5] "Say It Loud" not only marked a turning point in Black music but also influenced musicians from around the world—from Cameroon's Manu Dibango ("Soul Makossa") to Mick Jagger and Elvis Presley. Racial consciousness and identity became a theme in the music of the Temptations, Curtis Mayfield, and Sly and the Family Stone.

Brown's call-and-response with Black children imbued a message of Black pride to a new generation.[6] The opening exhortation "Uh! With your *bad* self!"—a common Black

American use of the English language to invert meaning—appropriated "bad" into something desirable (more than two decades before Michael Jackson declared himself "bad") and decreed a retort heard by all. Additionally, Brown's cultural appropriation of "Black" helped dismantle the constructed identities of Black people as Negroes or "colored." During the concurrent Civil Rights/Black Power movements, "Say It Loud" became the anthem of Black empowerment. Although the song cost Brown's crossover audience, he never regretted recording it because it "was badly needed at the time."[7]

Maurice White shared Brown's belief in the necessity of Brown's anthem. "Say It Loud" was necessary so that Black people ceased being ashamed of being Black and love themselves as Black people. Because of widespread colorism in Black communities, being called "black" was an insult. Brown's landmark cultural text served as a challenge to Black people against the denigration of blackness. Black pride would manifest in a variety of ways in the 1970s. Black American politicians, activists, educators, and artists built upon the achievements of the Civil Rights Movement and Black Power era by advancing new forms of confrontational protests such as Black feminism, expanding Black cultural spheres and expressions, and capitalizing on newly won legislative victories. The increase in Black empowerment spawned heightened Black pride.

Among Ramsey Lewis' many contributions to White was a book seized from a pile of giveaways in Lewis' home. *The Autobiography of Malcolm X* taught White that taking care of his body was a true expression of self-respect and love. White was convinced the story of Minister Malcolm's transformation spoke directly to him and inspired his own philosophical pursuits.[8]

While touring with the trio, White had a first-hand view of the social unrest that was taking place in America. He witnessed the riots occurring in cities as well as the violence police inflicted on Black Americans. As a young musician, White was victimized by the same systems of white supremacy and colorism that he first experienced as a child in Memphis. After leaving Memphis for Chicago, White immersed in reading, studying, and preparing to be the best musician he could be. He developed a plan to lead a band that created a musical experience that bestowed to humanity the promises of self-empowerment. White created EWF in 1970 to achieve his goal to render a service to humanity and uplift Black people. For nearly ten years White refined his vision and designated *TTWOTW*'s title track as EWF's national anthem.

EWF music in general and *TTWOTW* in particular offer inspirational messages of hope and aspiration sorely needed during any era, including today. EWF music is not overtly political but did respond to America's political and racial climate. EWF's music is *social* in that it relates to societal configurations and *communal* in creating shared experiences for listeners. In EWF's self-titled 1971 debut album, social messages are explicit and most of the seven songs address the need for social justice, compassion, and love. "This World Today" offers a plea for peace and positive change in a world of "troubled times":

> *Man fighting man, For no cause at all.*
> *And though it is wrong, the fighting goes on.*

*In this new world of suffering.*
*Love, peace of mind, should be our thing.*

EWF's "This World Today" is as vital today as it was in 1971. Many EWF songs are timeless because of their positive messages of love, spirituality, and self-empowerment. As EWF's melodies linger, their legacy continues to serve and uplift humanity as Maurice White envisioned. This analysis of EWF's *TTWOTW* demonstrates how EWF music connects people through their humanity and helps guide us through troubling times.

This short book encompasses my long journey with EWF's music. Writing this book has been a therapeutic labor of love and a much-needed respite during a global pandemic. However, long before I began researching and writing, the ideas of this project were being formulated. Since I attended my first of many EWF concerts in 1972, their music has remained at the center of my life and shaped some of my personal and professional relationships. I've played EWF's music on the radio stations I worked in Pennsylvania, Ohio, and Illinois. As a DJ, I played EWF hits such as "Mighty Mighty," "Reasons," and "Let's Groove" at parties and dance halls. I even presented a paper at an international academic conference that was inspired by the February 2016 passing of Maurice White and that month's Grammy Awards. In some ways this book represents the gestation of that project.

It is impossible to tell any story about EWF without chronicling the visionary leadership of White, so I draw heavily from his memoir published the same year as his death. I rely on his accounts of his early life while interrogating his claims and omissions in his professional life. Phillip Bailey's (2014) book also informs this work as do many of the hundreds of articles, broadcasts, and blogs/vlogs about EWF during the last fifty years. My April 2021 Zoom with Verdine White was an essential primary source in contextualizing this analysis. I've mapped the countless EWF television interviews and performances onto my own first-hand observations that include five concert performances. As an academic, I adhere to convention that serious examination extracts the work of scholars, cultural critics, and historians.

Most important, I write about music as a nonmusician who loves music. I write what I hear, see, and feel in music. I trust my sensory perceptions and hope they resonate with readers. It was love at first note when I attended my initial EWF concert at Philadelphia's Uptown Theater. This is the disposition that I proudly share the elements of my universe—EWF's *TTWOTW.*

# 1
# Yearnin'

## The Concept

The success of *TTWOTW*, like that of EWF, emerged in large part from Maurice White's unique and multifaceted musical vision or what he would eventually label, "The Concept." White's concept began in his dreams as a fantasy—of his own personal and professional desires. Always a work in progress, it took years of gestation for White to expand his personal vision into a concept for EWF. As early as 1967, White began committing his ideas to paper and sharing versions with anyone who could help him fulfill his vision. Although White credits the music of Sly Stone for inspiring his musical concept that would take years to flesh out, it dictated everything he did in his life. "I wanted a band that could express how I felt about life, how I felt about God, how I felt about identity, and how I felt about love."[1] This book's mapping of the evolution of White's concept—partially fulfilled in *TTWOTW*—begins with White's musical influences, associates, shifts in the country's political social environments, and changes in the music industry.

The earliest version (including sketches) of White's concept was a band of nine people that represented "clean living and be a force for good—no drugs, no booze, a respect for self, and a respect for your brother." White wanted to create and lead a band that performed various styles of music around the world representing "universal truths" and uplifting humanity by providing encouragement and peace.[2] Aware of the challenges he faced, White decided to leave The Ramsey Lewis Trio in 1969 to form EWF.

White also knew that his departure from a proven venture to start something from scratch required both a clear concept and the right musicians. White's memoir offers one of the few explications of his concept when he along with original EWF members Wade Flemons, Don Whitehead, Yackov Ben Israel, and Sherry Scott migrated from Chicago to Los Angeles in April 1970:

> My concept of [EWF] was that its music would render itself to humanity by encouraging an investment in the inner life. My self-love would project holistic and clean living through diet and no drugs. My plan was to exemplify a new brand of black masculinity rooted not in a super-black power thing but in dignity.[3]

### Yearnin' Learnin'

The origins of Maurice White's concept can be traced to his childhood desires (yearning) and the many lessons (learning) he absorbed over the first quarter century of his life. *TTWOTW*'s "Yearnin' Learnin'" encapsulates part of

White's personal journey and his professional desire to lead the creation of new styles of music for diverse audiences. In addition, musically, "Yearnin' Learnin'" contains some of the unique features that would become hallmarks of EWF's sound. One of these distinctive elements is the syncopated or "ragged" piano rhythm in the song's introduction.

Larry Dunn's syncopated ragtime stride-Fender Rhodes summons listeners to groove. As a jazz musician with Memphis and Chicago roots, White was intimately familiar with ragtime as a style of music originating from African American music and culture in the late nineteenth century that influenced twentieth-century jazz. In fact, as jazz surpassed ragtime in popularity in the 1920s, the ragtime revivals in the 1940s and 1950s probably did not elude the ears of Maurice White—and perhaps not even his young keyboardist, Larry Dunn.[4] Dunn had been playing jazz and popular music in Denver, Colorado, nightclubs since he was eleven and played keyboards in a Denver band he helped form, Friends and Love, which included future EWF members Phillip Bailey and Andrew Woolfolk. Dunn joined EWF in 1972 at age eighteen and played organ, synthesizer, piano, and clavinet. By the time he was twenty-one, Dunn served as the band's de facto musical director with a powerful creative influence on EWF typified on "Yearnin' Learnin'."

"Yearnin' Learnin'" opens with four faint bass drumbeats with the fifth beat accentuated by a dissonant F piano chord—the only time this chord is heard in the song. This dissonance compels listeners to focus and to groove (or stride) to the piano's rhythm. Dunn's syncopated rhythm embodies one of the key elements of funk music. The song's inclusion of syncopation, basslines, and drums places it squarely in the realm of funk. The opening drumbeats symbolize a very young boy nicknamed "Sandy" banging his toy drumsticks on his front porch in Memphis.

"Yearnin' Learnin'" kicks into high gear when Dunn's prefatory piano riff is capped by a blaring horn fanfare and drum fills that unleash the chorus:

> Stop! Look what's behind you. Fame & love gonna find
> you.
> We're just here to remind you. Yearn and learn is what
> you do.

The first line of the opening verse clearly signifies the ensuing story of a child. In this case, Maurice White's tale as a poor shy kid struggling in a Memphis housing project. However, this narrative also can apply to countless others and resonates with listeners. White's uncertain destiny and devotion to drumming and reading gave him a sense of what he could become. His lead vocal styling in "Yearnin' Learnin'" is reminiscent of one of his contemporary musical heroes, Sly Stone:

> Once upon a time, a child was born.
> With a light to carry on.

Maurice White was raised by his grandmother ("Mama") since the age of four after his birth mother ("Mother Dear") migrated from Memphis to Chicago to find better employment opportunities. Nicknamed "Sandy" because of his blonde hair, he was teased and bullied for having light skin and wearing second-hand clothes. Sandy's childhood joys came from his relationship with Mama, the church they attended, and the music they shared that became an obsession to White. Sandy enjoyed gospel music and sang in Rosehill Baptist Church's Rosehill Jubilettes, a gospel quartet that imitated the Soul Stirrers; pioneers of the quartet style of gospel, and a major influence on 1950s doo wop, 1960s soul, and Motown music. Sandy's early-age skepticism of the messages he heard delivered from the pulpit led to his abandonment of becoming a preacher to develop his own personal relationship with God and pursue music. His first real musical stint outside of the church came at the age of nine as a snare drummer with a local drum and bugle corps that he coveted primarily because of their uniforms.[5]

At the age of twelve, Sandy was invited by "Mother Dear" to visit her family in Chicago. White met his stepfather, Dr. Verdine Adams, and four younger brothers and sisters during his short stay. Following his return to Memphis, Sandy received the most prized possession of his young life—a bicycle gift from Dr. Adams. The bike symbolized a type of parental love from Dr. Adams, someone he barely knew. Sandy boasted with pride that the gift represented his connection to someone respectable in the Black community. Sandy also was developing an interest in music motivated by the diverse musical legacy in Memphis that included gospel, blues, rhythm & blues (R&B), and jazz.

As a teenager, White formed musical alliances with friends David Porter and Booker T. Jones. The trio formed doo-wop groups that sang under the streetlights and performed in junior high school talent shows. White's music instruction and performative training emerged from music education classes and talent shows at Booker T. Washington High School. Jones encouraged White—two years his senior, to focus on drums and jazz music: "My high school music buddies Maurice White and Richard Shann and I yearned to become proficient on our own instruments." He singles out White as his first peer who combined a commitment to creating music with virtuoso skills.[6] If White was not rehearsing or listening to music, he probably was beginning his lifelong love of reading that was inspired by a junior high school teacher.

White's popularity at school increased as his drumming improved. He also attributes his acceptance to his hair becoming more "kinkier" and less blonde. Sandy's bike facilitated his first job delivering papers—which became a necessity after Mama became ill. While delivering papers on the White (people) side of town one day, White received a beating from two White police officers. The policemen repeatedly called him a "nigger" and the incident haunted Sandy for several months. One of the first and important lessons Sandy learned was that police brutality and other abuses against Black people were routine occurrences in 1950s Memphis where Blacks were beginning to stand up for their rights. Sandy's first-hand experiences of racism shaped his attitude and understanding of his surroundings. He saw his beating as a type of backlash against the small gains of Blacks such as joining unions to obtain better jobs. The teenage Sandy also knew he would have to become the primary provider for his Mama and delivering papers would not be enough.

While in high school, White's first professional job was as a drummer with a group called Squash Campbell and the Mad

Lads. The gig taught him to be a more animated drummer and gave him the confidence to envisage himself as a future bandleader. Squash Campbell taught Sandy the valuable lesson that he could be a successful bandleader as long as he hustled jobs and kept a band working. Beyond music, White could afford to pay the rent and when he handled Mama's rent money, it was a rite of passage that signaled his manhood. He yearned to be a part of the music world he heard on the well-known Memphis radio station WDIA. White's musical partnerships with Squash Campbell, Booker T. Jones, and others solidified his passion for drumming and entertaining audiences.

A surprise visit by Mother Dear to Sandy's high school graduation led to a life-changing experience. White turned his mother's unexpected request to join her in Chicago into an opportunity to escape the racism of Memphis for better opportunities. White's belief that music saved him from the streets is reiterated in the second verse of "Yearnin' Learnin'":

*So the streets, he fled to shine*
*In a world of a different kind.*

Sandy was cognizant of Mama's dual distress over his leaving and support for his new life. White invoked his recollections of her encouragement throughout his professional journey and credits her for his own strength and positivity. Before reuniting with his new family in Chicago, White reluctantly said good-bye to his musical brothers, Booker T. Jones and David Porter. Jones drove White (and his girlfriend) to the train station for a solemn parting handshake turned hug, knowing their musical crossing had ended. Years later

Jones realized the necessity of their separation.[7] Had White remained in Memphis, he most likely would have worked at Satellite Records, a Memphis record label formed in 1957. His friend Booker T. Jones became a session musician at the label after playing saxophone on Satellite Records' first hit, "Cause I love You" by Carla and Rufus Thomas. Satellite Records became *Stax Records* in 1961 and one year later, Booker T. Jones formed his own band, Booker T. and the MGs, and released its mega-hit instrumental, "Green Onions."

There was no turning back or regrets for Sandy, just as the chorus and closing lines of "Yearnin' Learnin'" remind listeners:

*Stop! Look what's behind you.*
*Fame & love gonna find you . . .*

Sandy joined Mother Dear's family in Chicago and used the connections of his "Dad"—Dr. Verdine Adams, Sr., to obtain a job as an orderly at St. Luke's Presbyterian Hospital. When he learned his earnings would go to the Adams family household, White found a roommate, moved into an apartment, and purchased a drum set. Cognizant of greater career opportunities in medicine, White put drumming on hiatus to follow in Dad's footsteps to study medicine at Crane Junior College. His decision was due in part to his encounters with racism as a youth in Memphis and his awareness of the nation's racial realities: "as with everything else in America, whatever the ills may be of mainstream society, they're always worse for Black folks."[8]

White understood that doctors have status and respect in the community. He also savored the decent living a physician could have. Although his Chicago family lived in the recently built Henry Horner housing projects, they were clean, safe, and relatively free from the gangs, drugs, and crime that would permeate the city in the mid-1970s. Conversely, White realized it was Chicago with its fair share of thugs and societal ills. He quickly came to respect his dad who was a podiatrist and Renaissance man, spoke five different languages, and like Sandy, loved to read. Going to medical school was Sandy's way of embracing a full relationship with his dad, siblings, and Chicago. Ironically, Chicago's Crane Junior College would put Sandy in touch with a group of musicians that re-ignited his musical flames. As the chorus of "Yearnin' Learnin'" proclaims, "We're just here to remind you yearn and learn is what you do."

Just as he had done in his Memphis high school days, White formed friendships with a number of musicians, many of whom would remain in his orbit for the next thirty years. Most notably was Fred Humphrey, a pianist who White credits with helping him define himself as a musician and man. White began to question his medical aspirations after observing pianist Humphrey's student band practicing at Crane. The other musicians included Don Myrick (saxophone), Louis Satterfield (trombone), and Charles Handy (trumpet), all who would later join White's bands. But it was Humphrey, not surprisingly an avid reader, who had the greatest impact on Sandy. White credits Humphrey for transforming Sandy White of Memphis to Maurice White of Chicago.[9]

One book Humphrey gave White, Napoleon Hill's *The Law of Success*, became White's Bible. Published in 1928,

Hill's master course on positive thinking and achievement had a profound impact on White and his vision for EWF. The most prominent of Hill's sixteen lessons for White was the very first law: the necessity to have a plan for life. According to Hill, the path leading to success is prescribed for people who *yearn* with a burning desire that cannot be extinguished: "The object of your definite chief aim should become your 'hobby.' You should ride this 'hobby' continuously; you should sleep with it, eat with it, play with it, work with it, live with it and THINK with it."[10] As the following pages will uncover, music was White's "hobby." White describes his own thinking in words almost indistinguishable from Hill's: "It was like a bright light turned on in my consciousness, showing me that music would be my destiny. I knew that I would stay with it."[11]

White joined the Jazzmen sextet as drummer and left Crane Junior College to enroll in the Chicago Conservatory of Music. Much of his enduring musical work ethic began with the Jazzmen and consisted of rehearsing and practicing during the day, attending classes in the early evening, and performing blues, R&B, and jazz at Chicago's foremost jazz clubs at night. White's ethos is consistent with Napoleon Hill's philosophy of success that holds hard work and perseverance will beat talent and a poor work ethic every time. The fourth verse of "Yearnin' Learnin'" captures White's growing love for performing music accented by his Sly Stone-like ad-libs of "yeah" and "oh baby":

> *Gives your heart a special treat*
> *(Yeah) Clap your hands (Oh baby) stomp your feet . . .*

The vocals ascend on "so we learn" with Phillip Bailey's falsetto adding, "yeah yeah yeah yeah." Although Phillip Bailey is known as EWF's primary falsetto vocalist, by the time *TTWOTW* was recorded, Maurice White had expanded his range from tenor to falsetto and their vocal vamps are stacked in the repeated chorus lines of "Yearnin' Learnin'."

Funk music scholar Rickey Vincent acknowledges James Brown as the initiator of the emphatic first note or beat in a measure as fundamental to funk.[12] "Yearnin' Learnin'" creates a funk-intensive groove with beats that emphasize the "one" along with strong guitar riffs, Verdine White's electric basslines, and horns that set the song on fire. *TTWOTW* was the first EWF album to feature a large horn section consisting of trombonist George Bohanon, Oscar Brashear on trumpet, and saxophonist Ernie Watts.[13] Their blazing staccato and rhythmic sound distinguishes EWF's horns from the harmonies of Chicago's notable horn section of Lee Loughnane, Walter Parazaider, and Jimmy Pankow.[14]

Booker T. Jones' memoir calls friend and bandmate Maurice White's departure from Memphis to Chicago the first significant separation in his life. Yet Jones considered the parting necessary because neither musician would have achieved their full capabilities together, since they supported and limited each other. Their true brotherhood became apparent to Jones in 1976 when he first listened to the title selection of *TTWOTW*: "Maurice was doing the work of his life" as was intended (by God)[15] Jones' assessment is supported by a major theme in both Hill's book and "Yearnin' Learnin'": identify what you really want, set your mind to that goal, and invigorate your life's work with study and practice. For White, who co-wrote "Yearnin' Learnin'" with Charles Stepney and Phillip Bailey, the aim to be a great musician would require more than dedication and hard work. White also wanted the song's theme of self-empowerment to inspire listeners to develop a goal and remain committed to it. White's future experiences in Chicago and Los Angeles produced successes, setbacks, and learning opportunities that were essential for developing a successful plan for life.

# 2
# Learnin'

## Chicago

White's concept for EWF began to take shape during his later years in Chicago. By the time he relocated to Los Angeles, it continued to evolve as a synthesis of diverse musical styles and philosophies, spiritual ideas, lessons of personal growth and fulfillment, and social awareness. The foundation of his concept to render a service to humanity through music was consistent with Napoleon Hill's lesson to "render more service than that which you are paid and you will soon be paid for more than you render." As a bandleader, White personified Hill's notions of leadership and service: "You can never become a Leader without doing more than you are paid for and you cannot become successful without developing leadership in your chosen occupation."[1]

Musically, White's vision embodied such characteristics as innovative melodies, stylistic diversity—including African and Latin rhythms, layered sounds and voices, heavy percussion and horns, lush orchestra arrangements, and positive messages. Performatively, White's concept progressed from basic staging and organic performances to vibrant theatrical spectacles by a collaborative creative ensemble of artists who turned their diverse ways of life and spiritualities into communal experiences. Because Maurice White's concept evolved alongside various band members' progression for several years, he is not seen in the same artistic prodigy as a Stevie Wonder, Prince, or even James Brown. Although White developed his concept for EWF, it was inspired by Mama, Napoleon, Hill, and numerous musicians. To the degree in which EWF fulfilled White's concept, resulted in part from collaborative creative responses to societal conditions and creative exigencies. White's dynamic concept and its manifestation in *TTWOTW* can be tracked through White's professional trajectory and contextualized in America's troubled racial history, and trends in the music industry.

White left the Jazzman in 1963 when he landed a job as a session musician at Black-owned Vee-Jay Records. His recollections of the first day on the job were not musical but sorrow throughout the studio following the murder of four little Black girls at the bombing of the Sixteenth Street Baptist Church in Birmingham, Alabama. The White supremacist terror attack came only eighteen days after Dr. King led a large nonviolent march on Washington, D.C. A couple of months later, the nation mourned the assassination of President John F. Kennedy. Because horrific tragedies were not new to Black people, most Black musicians like White had to compartmentalize such events and focus on their music.

One notable exception was vocalist Nina Simone, who confronted racial oppression on a regular basis in the Deep South's chitlin' circuit—the training ground for many Black musicians. Simone wrote and recorded "Mississippi Goddamn" for the burgeoning civil rights movement shortly after the church bombing. Ironically, her first song for the movement was rarely played on the radio and largely unavailable in the South because of record industry distribution boycotts. Simone would record other civil rights anthems such as "Young, Gifted and Black." It would be a couple of years later before Maurice White would contribute musically to the movement. However, his first major professional musical success came at the age of twenty-two as drummer on Betty Wright's (1963) hit single, "You're No Good"—a feat he and bandmate Louis Satterfield would parlay into additional musical achievements.

Chicago's South Michigan Avenue was known as "Record Row" because of its ten-block stretch where several independent record companies produced blues, rhythm and blues (R&B), jazz, and soul music from the late 1950s to the mid-1970s. The most prominent of these companies was Chess Records. Billy Davis, an A&R (Artist & Repertoire) person at Chess, hired White and Satterfield as studio musicians. Davis became a mentor to White at the legendary R&B label. Besides absorbing music and recording lessons from Davis and other well-known musicians who recorded at Chess, White also learned the importance of self-assertiveness from the many Black musicians who lacked agency and self-sufficiency. In this sense he followed Hill's law of self-confidence as the product of knowledge: "Know yourself, know how much you know (and how little)."[2]

Other lessons White discerned from *The Law of Success* were to stay independent and refine his craft. White's pledge not to become dependent on, nor a victim of Chess Records was evident during his studies at the Chicago Conservatory of Music. White improved his technique and facilitated associations outside of the Chess orbit. After his stint with the Jazzmen, he formed Quartet 4, named after the Modern Jazz Quartet. Yet it was Chess Records that provided White with numerous influencers such as Curtis Mayfield, who inspired White on the power of consciousness-raising through song. White branded songs by Curtis Mayfield and the Impressions such as "Keep on Pushing" and "People Get Ready" as "gentle short sermons."[3] White topped his earlier notoriety at Vee-Jay Records after drumming on Fontella Bass' "Rescue Me," one of the best-selling records in Chess' history. The 1965 crossover hit arose from a Chess studio session known as "woodshedding", intense practicing with the hope that something creatively special would result. The song features Bass' riveting soprano lead, White's drums in perfect sync with Louis Satterfield's bubbly bass, an unknown background vocalist named Minnie Riperton who participated in electrifying call-and-response chorusing, and Charles Stepney on vibes.[4] White and Stepney apparently used woodshedding during Caribou Ranch recording sessions for *TTWOTW*. The frequent call-and-responses on the album comprise one of the creative touches from the 1965 hit to adorn EWF's landmark album ten years later. Stepney, who co-produced *TTWOTW* along with Maurice

White, may have had the strongest influence on *TTWOTW* (besides White).

Charles Stepney was a brilliant pianist/vibraphonist and writer who used his classical music training to integrate orchestrations into popular music. His lavish orchestral arrangements embody one aspect of his immense imprint on *TTWOTW*. Ramsey Lewis, Verdine White, and others have compared Stepney's talent to Quincy Jones. Verdine White even characterizes the arranger/producer as EWF's George Martin.

Although White's collaboration with Stepney began at Chess, Stepney's work with EWF began in 1973 with the band's fifth studio album, *Open Our Eyes* (*OOE*), recorded at Colorado's Caribou Ranch. White sought his mentor's guidance in expanding EWF's diverse sound. Despite Stepney's limited impact on *OOE* (compared to *TTWOTW*) and disdain for Caribou Ranch, White's first call in crafting the soundtrack was to Stepney who reluctantly joined EWF at Caribou to record *TTWOTW*. After initially cautioning White against doing the soundtrack, Stepney agreed to serve as co-producer. Sharing Stepney's view that a film's fate can determine that of the soundtrack, White's confidence in producer/director Sig Shore was based on his previous film *Superfly*.

White focused on what he could control (the music) and placed his faith in the music of EWF. White decided to deviate from the traditional approach to doing a soundtrack to ensure that EWF's concept was reflected in the score. Instead of composing music that reinforced the film, EWF composed music for an album that was consistent with White's vision for EWF without deviating from their customary themes. Stepney not only produced and arranged *TTWOTW* but also remained by White's side throughout the process. White respected Stepney enough to allow him to coach the entire band, including White, who saw himself as the quarterback.

In the documentary *Shining Stars: The Official Story of Earth, Wind & Fire*, Phillip Bailey credits Stepney for being able "to write it, arrange it, play it, and show us how to sing it and tell us when it's wrong."[5] Although every song on *TTWOTW* was composed differently, the music always preceded the lyrics. The band followed a process of developing skeletons of songs and taking those ideas into the studio to allow for improvisation. There may be some truth to the criticisms of the band's songwriting, but quality musicianship and production overcame sporadic writing flaws. Each song could be recorded as many as eight to ten times and Maurice usually picked the best take during mixing. This gave Stepney a solid foundation to add orchestrations which would be followed by keyboard and synthesizer overdubs. Stepney brought sophisticated symphonic textures and eloquent chord changes to EWF's palpably unique sonic style. As I will discuss later, Stepney brought musical interludes that became a staple of EWF albums and *TTWOTW* in particular. But it was Stepney's masterful orchestral arrangements that were both unique to popular music of the era and a novelty to Chess Records.

Marshall Chess, the son of Chess Records co-founder Leonard Chess, enlisted the Chicago musician to form a psychedelic rock/soul band for the Chess sub-label, Cadet Concept. Stepney created Rotary Connection as part of a strategy to broaden Chess' R&B brand. For the experimental band's first album, Stepney made the unusual move to deploy the string section of the Chicago Symphony Orchestra. Stepney also brought to Rotary Connection's lineup his friend and Chess session musician Phil Upchurch, as well as young Chicago native Minnie Riperton's five-octave vocal range. The six albums that Rotary Connection recorded under Stepney's guidance were ground-breaking although not commercially successful. In a 2021 tribute to Stepney, writer Paul Bowler described Rotary Connection's sound as "a glorious fusion of styles made essential by the simpatico nature of Stepney's lush string arrangements and [Minnie] Riperton's multi-octave, quasi-operatic vocals."[6] Stepney was also producing and arranging for the soul group The Dells; soul, folk, and jazz guitarist Terry Callier; and The Ramsey Lewis Trio. He would later produce Riperton's debut album, *Come to My Garden*.

Another Chess collaborator, Billy Stewart, impacted White as a drummer, producer, and performer. Stewart, a heavy (300+lb) singer who White describes as an agile "performer unequaled by anyone," did microphone stand maneuvers alongside his idiosyncratic improvisational technique of doubling-up, scatting his vocals, and trilling his lips.[7] Stewart traced his unique vocal style of studdering and rapid-fire explosion of words to his early interest in calypso.[8] White contends the vocalist—nicknamed "motormouth", taught him how to draw the best out of a rhythm section. White showcased his potential as a drummer on two of Stewart's biggest (and self-written) hits, "I Do Love You" and "Sitting in the Park," yet maintained that Stewart's most important album was *Unbelievable*, the 1966 collection of standards. The first single released from that album was Stewart's radical interpretation of George Gershwin's "Summertime," a Top ten hit on both the pop and R&B charts. The recording introduced national audiences to Stewart's unique scatting style, and to assiduous listeners—White's elegant drumming. The song fused the artificial boundaries between jazz, R&B, and popular music to become a career-defining moment for the 28-year-old singer.[9] Like Stewart, Ramsey Lewis was a musician whose blend of jazz and popular music had a profound impact on Maurice White and ultimately, EWF.

Ramsey Lewis met White at Chess when the quiet drummer posed questions to Lewis about the music business, staging, and performance.[10] Lewis enlisted the 25-year-old White to join his successful jazz trio in 1966 following the departures of drummer Redd Holt and bassist Eldee Young who left to form their own band, the Young-Holt Trio. Lewis recruited White and Cleveland Eaton because neither required extensive musical training and all three shared common roots in gospel music. Lewis found White to be both technically proficient and aware of the various styles of drumming that had gone before him.[11] Instead of imitating the former trio's sound, the new trio fostered a sound of their own. White's unique style of drumming was one of many attributes that White would incorporate into his own concept for EWF. These practices included crafting slight modifications to EWF's sound following personnel changes and incorporating African themes into their sound. White would expand the latter to include EWF members donning West African garb and symbols and imagery from North Africa on EWF albums.

## The Ramsey Lewis Trio

White's first album with The Ramsey Lewis Trio was "Wade in the Water" (1966). His first taste of public acclaim with the trio ensued from the single "Hold It Right There," which earned a Grammy. But another single from that album, the entrancing "Wade in the Water," became a bigger hit and cemented White's spot in the trio. Beyond the gold record, the trio's instrumental version became an anthem to the modern civil rights movement. The song not only gave White a connection to the civil rights movement's struggle for justice and equality for African Americans during the 1950s and 1960s, but also initiated White's interest in his motherland of Africa. The song's depiction of the Israelites' escape from Egypt allegedly inspired Harriet Tubman to use the song to instruct slaves to move off the trail and into the water to elude the slavers' dogs.

Touring with The Ramsey Lewis Trio also gave White time to feed his love of reading. Lewis gave White his copy of *The Autobiography of Malcolm X,* which motivated the drummer to stop eating pork and question his Christian roots. Although White still considered *The Law of Success* his bible, reading *The Prophet* gave White the mystic he craved in Kahlil Gibran. White's appreciation for Africa as the mother of civilization grew as did his awareness of African influences on Black American cultures. Over time, White recognized that all Black American music is rooted in African conceptual approaches to music. White became fascinated with Egypt and its relations to such ageless religions as Buddhism, Islam, and Christianity. As his own spirituality shifted from Christianity to mysticism, White incorporated mystic themes into EWF's music and Egyptian symbols such as the Ankh and Eye of the Horus into EWF's album designs. White's affinity for North Africa motivated him to take the entire band and crew on a sightseeing getaway to Cairo, Egypt, in 1979. The most immediate impact of his three-year stint with Ramsey Lewis was his use of an African thumb piano, known as a kalimba, which became a signature feature of EWF's music.

White was invested in the Black arts and Afrocentric movements that were developing across the country. These undertakings filled part of the void left by the absence of radical and grassroots organizations that lobbied for political and social change in the sixties. When not on the road with Ramsey Lewis, White was a frequent visitor to Chicago's Affro-Arts Theater where he heard such musicians as Oscar Brown, Jr., Syl Johnson, and former Sun Ra trumpeter Phil Cohran, who operated the Artistic Heritage Ensemble out of the theater. Cohran was the first to amplify an African thumb piano as a member of Sun Ra's Arkestra in the late 1950s, calling it a "Frankiphone" (named after his mother). White saw Cohran play the instrument and developed a strong affinity for the dual primitive and futuristic melodic tones of the mbira, or its more popular name, kalimba.

Mbira is a family of musical instruments, traditional to the Shona people of Zimbabwe. All consist of a wooden board (often fitted with a resonator) with attached staggered metal tines, played by holding the instrument in the hands and plucking the tines with the thumbs and right and left forefingers. Musicologists classify it as a lamellaphone and part of the plucked idiophone line of musical instruments.

There are many kinds of mbira in Eastern and Southern Africa and in the mid-1950s were the basis for the development of the kalimba, a westernized version designed and marketed by the ethnomusicologist Hugh Tracey.[12] Various kinds of plucked idiophones and lamellaphones have existed in Africa for thousands of years. These metal-tined instruments traveled all across the continent, becoming popular among the Shona of Zimbabwe (from which the word mbira comes) and other indigenous groups in Zimbabwe and Mozambique. Kalimba-like instruments came to exist from the northern reaches of North Africa to the southern extent of the Kalahari Desert and from the east to the west coasts. White found the African origins of the Kalimba appealing, purchased one and practiced on it regularly.

During rehearsals with The Ramsey Lewis Trio, White experimented with the different textures it brought to rhythms. His attraction to the kalimba embraced the African musical tenet that approached the singing or the playing of any instrument in a percussive manner. Lewis encouraged the reserved White to incorporate the kalimba into the trio's show. Despite his reluctance, he conceded and was so impressed by audiences' responses to his performance that he kept playing it. White has rightfully earned the notoriety of the kalimba's prominence in Black popular music. Although White never played with Cohran, he was influenced by the avant-garde musician in more ways than he publicly acknowledges. Beyond Cohran's introduction of the kalimba to White, there are other aspects of Cohran's musical and personal philosophies that are remarkably similar to parts of what became White's concept for EWF.

Phil Cohran was an innovative, if not an eccentric, musician who personified an Afrocentric approach to uplifting Black American life and intellect while resisting countervailing political and market forces. He joined Sun Ra's Arkestra in 1960 and played mostly trumpet and occasional string and percussion instruments. When Sun Ra left Chicago in 1961, Cohran remained in the city and formed the Artistic Heritage Ensemble (AHE) which released several albums on Cohran's Zulu label. Cohran recruited AHE members from the Chess Records house band, including some future members of a local band called The Salty Peppers which morphed into EWF. Cohran is also known for founding the Affro-Arts Theater in 1967. He claims to have taught music to the White brothers in their youth. In one interview he asserts that Verdine White played with the AHE and Maurice tried, but didn't make it because "he couldn't hold the rhythm. We had a rhythmic system that demanded perfect rhythm."[13] Regardless of the veracity of Cohran's claims about Maurice and Verdine White, there is no dispute that Maurice White shared Cohran's belief in the edifying purposes of music by imparting profound meanings to audiences.

White also emulated Cohran's demand for disciplined musicians who could express his own ideas and what he felt were the original purposes of music. Cohran, like White, insisted that his musicians be multifaceted performers while advocating a healthy lifestyle and spiritual development.[14] Cohran was a vegetarian who shared his interests in world religions, spirituality, Egyptology, and astrology with visitors to the Affro-Arts Theater.[15] As I will demonstrate in later chapters, White would adopt a similar approach to leading members of EWF following his departure from The Ramsey Lewis Trio.

White's last album with The Ramsey Lewis Trio was the 1969 release, *Another Voyage*, supervised by Charles Stepney. One song composed by White and the only Ramsey Lewis recording to showcase him on the kalimba was "Uhuru," which means freedom in Swahili. "Uhuru" opens with Cleveland Eaton's funky upright bass which provides the foundation for the song's up-tempo rhythm, dominated by the kalimba's sharp notes with a slight discordant edge, and followed by a slowly decaying pure tone.[16] White's kalimba drives the melody as he adds drum fills, cymbal brushes, and tambourine shakes to the trio's supportive chants, hollas, and handclaps heard in the background. White credits both the instrument and his mentor for helping him overcome his shyness and providing additional substance to his musical vision. White's Afrocentric sensibility displayed in "Uhuru" via his kalimba is incorporated in varying degrees into most EWF's albums.

In the self-titled 1971 debut on Warner Bros., EWF introduces White's kalimba on the closing track, "Bad Tune." The kalimba is featured throughout the 30-second intro and adds a crispy texture to the nearly 10-minute instrumental (credits list it as an "electric kalimba"). Although the follow-up album, *The Need of Love*, also credits Maurice White on drums, percussion, vocals, and kalimba, there are no audible indicators of the kalimba on any of the five songs. EWF's third album and first on Columbia Records (1972), *Last Days and Time (LDAT)*, showcases White's shimmering kalimba chords on "Power," an aptly titled 8-minute instrumental that earned staying power after *LDAT* when the song was paired with "Africano" (from *TTWOTW*) for EWF's live concert openings in the mid-1970s. "Power" was also the song used to open most EWF live performances before 1975. White's Hugh Tracey treble kalimba provides a colorful rhythm on the Latin-laced "Evil" from EWF's fourth album, *Head to the Sky* (*HTTS*). White's kalimba narrative is the theme of "Kalimba Story" from EWF's fifth album, *Open Our Eyes* (*OOE*). As lead vocalist, White conveys EWF's desire to introduce new styles of music through the kalimba. *OOE* also features White's kalimba throughout the instrumental "Drum Song," which connects listeners to Africa through the percussive power of drums. The kalimba provides the rhythmic melody of "Drum Song" as White jumps octaves and provides a lightness that counters the weighty drumming resulting in what I feel is an enlightening spiritual aura.

## Africano

*TTWOTW* picks up where "Drum Song" leaves off by providing a striking African ambience in "Africano." Written by Larry Dunn and Maurice White, "Africano" is a 5-minute instrumental that bestows a vivid African aural excursion that begins with a serene flute solo by Andrew Woolfolk. At :23, mellow background crooning escorts gentle plucking strokes from White's kalimba, which continue until the flute and kalimba do a few bars of call-and-response. The kalimba provides a fitting entry to almost any African landscape before it yields to the full band. The peaceful 1:17 introduction closes with a slow fade of the flute allowing the song to shift tempo with a thunderous percussion burst of congas, drums, and cowbell. Soaring horns punctuated by Dunn's piercing Minimoog licks establish the song's pulsating rhythm. The harmonic counterpoints of the staccato horns merge with Al McKay's rhythm guitar to insinuate rapid movements through the motherland before giving way to Woolfolk's alto sax. Just as "Drum Song" connoted a spiritual awakening, "Africano" instills powerful inflections of African pride.

Maurice White, like Phil Cohran, did not play traditional African music and both used their kalimbas as references to Africa. Without understating the varieties of African music, most use a multiplicity of sounds with short melodies often repeated. "Africano" captures the African polyrhythms that have been part of the Black music tradition throughout the twentieth century. The drum provides the heartbeat, the soul if you will—of most African communities. Drums have been an intrinsic part of African life for centuries and for countless generations, an instrument used to communicate and celebrate various aspects of life. In Western cultures drumming is usually about entertainment. In Africa, drums hold a deeper, symbolic, and historical significance. The drumming in "Africano" creates the fast-paced, upbeat, rhythmic tempo that signifies most African music. In addition, if drums are about communication and music, the drums in "Africano" signify African power more than anything else.

As noted earlier, "Africano" was paired fittingly with "Power" as the opening song for EWF concerts in the mid-to-late 1970s. The most celebrated version of "Africano/Power" was the 5:44 opening track on *Gratitude*, EWF's follow-up to *TTWOTW*. The first minute and one-half is a rendition of "Power," leaving the remaining 4 minutes to "Africano." In both live and studio versions, "Africano" is one of EWF's finest use of complex horn assimilation into the arrangement by playing fluid secondary melodies before vaulting into the foreground. According to White, EWF had been developing "Africano/Power" on-stage and in the studio since 1971 and describes the live version as a synthesis of jazz fusion, Afro-Cuban jazz, funk, and even more power their fans heard on any EWF record.[17]

## Crafting the Concept

As White toured with Ramsey Lewis he noticed a unique sense of showmanship that Lewis expected from his trio, which was rare in jazz performances. Similarly, White was aware of the divisions between jazz and blues and R&B that meant most R&B musicians did not possess the training or complexity to play jazz. Similarly, unlike most jazz musicians, White and a small cadre of his contemporaries had already demonstrated their ambidexterity playing jazz and R&B. White also discovered that many of the trio's fans were not jazz enthusiasts. Lewis recalls the shy drummer making note of these in a journal. Some were musical, while others were spiritual or philosophical. One of the most important of these notes was White's revelation that college students were looking for something different—a new, inspiring sound.[18] White integrated this observation into the core of his developing concept for a band. These and other observations would undergird White's musical philosophy and shape EWF's success in traversing long-standing musical boundaries.

Although touring with The Ramsey Lewis Trio on college campuses and in luxuriant venues around the world was enlightening, they could not shield White from the realities of race in America. Like many Americans, he watched in horror the riots in American cities. White's arrest along with bandmember Cleveland Eaton in Indianapolis for inviting two White women to their room bore a sad reminder of the country's racist legacy. White's reflections in jail about the fates of the Scottsboro Boys and Emmitt Till conveyed warnings of the dangers of personal associations that would carry over into his leadership of EWF. White also adopted Lewis' belief that Black men should be dignified, respectful, and strong.

This was the type of Black masculinity that White would incorporate into his concept for EWF. White also parlayed his own acceptance of Lewis' leadership, both musically and personally, as a prerequisite for membership in his band. This would prove to be difficult, at least initially.

Another important lesson from Napoleon Hill that White both needed and affirmed in his work with Ramsey Lewis was positivity. White needed a positive mindset to deal with America's oppressive racial dynamics. In order to accomplish that, White drew from his positive social interactions outside of the United States while on tour with Ramsey Lewis.

White's autobiography recalls affectionately his tours through Asia where he developed a deep appreciation for

Asian cultures. Beginning in Tokyo and in various other cities, White developed a fondness for Asian people who he described simply as "beautiful." He relished not only Asian audiences' appreciation of The Ramsey Lewis Trio's music, but how they were mesmerized by his drumming. White's major takeaway was music's ability to transcend cultural differences and provide bridges between people.[19] He expresses this sentiment in the third verse of "Yearnin' Learnin'": "He just felt so, good inside. Watchin' people come alive. Throbbin' rhythm, stir your soul. Melodies of joy unfold."

While in Asia, White studied Buddhism and connected it to many of the tenets of Christianity from his days in Church as a youth in Memphis. Buddhism steered him to other esoteric religions and ultimately to his belief in universal spirituality. Contrary to White's perceptions of Asian ways of life of minimalism, less materialism, and order, he found social conditions in the United States in disarray. Under Lewis' tutelage, White connected with people who sought some semblance of enlightenment amid the chaos in the nation. White's developing positivity was challenged by racial unrest, the Vietnam War, and the 1968 assassinations of Bobby Kennedy and Dr. King.

White also was bothered by the prevalence of alcohol and drugs inside and outside of the music industry. He wrestled with the addictions of Charlie Parker, Billie Holiday, John Coltrane, and was particularly stung by the 1968 heroin overdose of the popular young soul singer Frankie Lymon. In December 1969, two young Black Panther Party leaders, Fred Hampton and Mark Clark, were assassinated in their apartment by Chicago police during an FBI-coordinated raid. Although a federal grand jury refuted police's self-defense claims, there were no indictments in the killings—an all too familiar outcome of policing and criminal justice for Black Americans. I point to this latter event because it may have contributed to White's decision more than a year later to do the music for a Melvin Van Peebles film that took on policy brutality and included a character who was a member of the Black Panther Party (BPP). BPP co-founder Huey P. Newton would celebrate the film's Black revolutionary themes and declared "*Sweetback*" required viewing for BPP members. Like so many Americans in the late 1960s and early 1970s, White needed answers and a framework to better understand himself and the world around him.

One of White's immediate responses was to stay clear of drugs and further his own health and diet regimen that was inspired by Ramsey Lewis and Malcolm X's autobiography. Despite White's disapproval of drug use by musicians, he cites Sly and the Family Stone as a strong musical influence and praises Sly directly for liberating music in ways that gave him the confidence to advance his own distinct musical ideas. For White, Dr. King's dreams of an integrated America were both expressed in the songs of Sly and the Family Stone and on display in the band's racial and gender diversity. White's memoir concedes that before discovering Sly and the Family Stone, his own plan for becoming a great musician was incomplete. At this time, it is likely that White's unfinished blueprint was as much about his own personal growth as it was about music. White sought a better understanding of his psychological makeup through astrology.

White's studies in astrology led him to seek specific knowledge of the planetary positions of his chart from well-known Chicago astrologer James Black. In their meeting, Black informed White that his astrological chart reveals only his natural tendencies, but what he did with the information will determine his life. White learned his chart had no water which apparently meant a noticeable lack of emotion that he compensated for with a loving relationship with his music. His goal to become a bandleader was predicated on personal refinements such as increasing his emotional intelligence in his interactions with colleagues. Although White would continue to struggle with his emotional detachment when he became the leader of EWF, he embraced another philosophy and fused it with his concept.

As most of Black America's hopes for achieving racial justice and equality that emanated from the 1960s were being thwarted, many Black Americans shifted their attention from politics and civil rights to Black culture and identity. "Black is Beautiful" began as an expression and emerged into a philosophy that signaled an appreciation of an African past as a worthy legacy and inspired cultural pride in Black achievements. The philosophy manifested in the arts, scholarship, and other creative endeavors in support of a cultural revolution. "Black is Beautiful" also included emotional and psychological well-being by affirming natural hairstyles and the variety of skin tones, hair textures, and other physical characteristics found in Black communities. Like many other cultural producers and artists of the era, Maurice White molded his personal philosophies through this broad cultural prism and developed a self-enlightened consciousness of healthy living, cultural awareness, and Afrocentric thinking:

> It was not a militant Black power thing, but a place of Black awareness, teaching us to fall in love with our culture, giving us an understanding of our rightful place on the planet and of ourselves. It was more than dashikis and Afros.[20]

White is making an important distinction between Black is Beautiful—which he favored—and Black Power—a political slogan used by many Black Americans to achieve self-determination for Black people. Both expressions made their way through the United States in the late 1960s and early 1970s. Black is Beautiful emerged from the Black Power movement and it quickly permeated the American cultural mainstream through the adoption of Afro hairstyles and Afrocentric fashion. Black Power was advocated primarily, but not exclusively by Black activists and radicals such as Stokely Carmichael. The differences between the cultural and political movements are not as clear as many would believe because they are not mutually exclusive. Both advocated for Black pride and self-determination, despite those who associated Black Power with separatism and violence. As an artist, White favored Black is Beautiful because he realized that Black and White people needed each other. Yet the perceived tensions between the two movements were real and generated friction between White and some of his original members of EWF who were more militant in their racial thinking.

Following his 1969 meeting with astrologer James Black, White acted upon Napoleon Hill's blended lessons of (financial) independence, initiative, and leadership: "*Initiative and Leadership* are associated terms in this lesson for the reason that *Leadership* is essential for the attainment of *Success,* and *Initiative* is the very foundation upon which this necessary quality of *Leadership* is built."[21] White's desire to have something of his own apart from Ramsey Lewis led him to initiate a collaboration with musical colleagues Louis Satterfield, Chuck Handy, and others such as emerging keyboardist and arranger, Donny Hathaway. The eight Chicago-based musicians recorded several songs and released a single titled "La La Time (Part 1)" on Capitol Records under a band White named The Salty Peppers. Despite the large group of experienced musicians and an up-and-coming Hathaway, "La La Time" was a marginal hit in the Midwest and the flip side "Uh Huh Yeah" bombed. The songs lacked polish and profound messages. White remained undeterred and drew inspiration from the successful Black male creative leaders he knew (Billy Davis, Charles Stepney, Ramsey Lewis, etc.) as well as from Napoleon Hill's law of positivity.

White shared his embryonic concept with Ramsey Lewis and long-time Memphis friend, David Porter. Although Porter found White's idea well thought out, Lewis thought it was foolish to even consider leaving the trio at the peak of its success to form a band that sought to uplift people through diverse musical genres. Lewis' negative reaction to White's plan to perform pop, Latin, R&B, jazz, and soul was surprising given his success at mixing a variety of genres into his jazz repertoire. On the heels of his mega-hit "The 'In' Crowd," Lewis faced backlash from the jazz establishment for appealing to broader audiences.

White claimed his vision and the universal truths it represented was more important than the music. A far greater test than White's goal to uplift humanity was the extent to which he would allow his band to express how *they* too felt about life. Reconciling this tension would go a long way in determining the success of White's concept. Another obstacle White faced came from another lesson from *The Law of Success*, to save money. It would take years after establishing EWF before White became an effective manager of his financial resources. His decision to leave Chicago, Chess Records, and The Ramsey Lewis Trio was ridiculed not only by Ramsey Lewis but also by musical associates like Pete Cosey, who played guitar on the Salty Pepper recordings and told him he was making a huge mistake. One of the few musicians to support for White's plan to move to Los Angeles and form a band was his long-time Memphis friend David Porter. Porter listened to White describe the musical aspects of his concept and responded with a simple affirmation, "I know you can do it."[22] White's decision also was supported by the most important person in his life at that time, Mother Dear. Although White knew Lewis questioned his plan, the two parted ways amicably only to reunite five years later to collaborate on an album that boosted both of their careers.

Around the same time of his departure from Lewis' trio, White joined Lewis, Phil Upchurch, and Charles Stepney (producer) in a 1969 recording session at Chicago's Tel-Mar Studios for Minnie Riperton's debut solo album. For reasons that may forever remain unknown, White's autobiography ignores his work on Riperton's debut, *Come to My Garden*. Even though the two worked together at

Chess, White's omission of Riperton is paradoxical given his acknowledgment of the influential roles of so many other Chess collaborators.[23] It is also possible that White did not want to take a back seat to a female musician's work. Yet at the time White worked on his memoir, Riperton had firmly established herself as a musical icon whose career and life ended way too soon. As White was strategizing his own undertaking, perhaps Riperton's desire to pursue a solo career may have quenched any partnerships between the two musicians.

Today, *Come to My Garden* is considered by many as an artistic masterpiece because of Riperton's vocal elegance and Charles Stepney's orchestral arrangements. The album was not a commercial success, but "Les Fleurs," co-written by Stepney and Riperton's fiancé Richard Rudolph, is the album's most memorable song. White's drumming contributes to the song's orchestral paradise—from his brisk shuffle to resounding crescendos—a dynamic he and Stepney would deploy in *TTWOTW*. Interestingly, Ramsey Lewis originally wrote a more refined instrumental version, "Le Fleur" for his 1968 *Maiden Voyage* album. By the time *Come to My Garden* was released in late 1970, White had named and relocated his new band to Los Angeles.[24]

# 3
# Revolving Doors

Don't be afraid of a little opposition. Remember that the kite of success generally rises against the wind of adversity—not with it.

*Napoleon Hill[1]*

## Los Angeles

In April 1970, Maurice White led a caravan of select members of The Salty Peppers (minus Donny Hathaway and younger brother Fred who played tambourine on "La La Time") to Los Angeles under the name "Earth, Wind and Fire" apparently induced by James Black's interpretation of White's astrological charts. White was joined by Chicago jazz vocalist Sherry Scott along with Don Whitehead (acoustic and electric piano), Wade Flemons (vocals and electric piano), and another Chicago recruit, percussionist Yakov Ben Israel (Phillard Williams). White held auditions in Los Angeles that yielded guitarist Michael Beal and a three-piece horn section (trumpeter Leslie Drayton, tenor saxophonist Chester Washington, and trombonist Alex Thomas) to give him a bigger sound. However, all but two (Maurice and Verdine White) of these original EWF members would be replaced in eighteen months and long before *TTWOTW* was released in 1975.

White was confident that Capitol Records would offer a contract to his band based on the regional success of "La La Time." The 28-year-old believed a new name, some new musicians, the success of Sly and the Family Stone, and LA's eclectic music would allow his concept to flourish. Unfortunately, White was reminded of the music industry's inequitable treatment of Black musicians when Capitol refused to pick up the band's contract. White failed to fully reconcile Capitol's decision with the (modest) gains he observed Black Americans making in certain segments of American society. White faced additional challenges during his first two years in LA. Most of the setbacks related to EWF personnel changes and record label management and support.

EWF needed a bass player and White called his younger brother Verdine to leave Chicago to join the band. Verdine put off college and joined his brother in LA. Verdine began playing the upright bass as a pre-teen, worked under the tutelage of Louis Satterfield, and was a classically trained musician with the Chicago Symphony Orchestra. At the tender age of nineteen, he had never been outside of Illinois. and did not fully understand his brother's "concept." He saw it as something that belonged to Maurice and had to "think it through" before embracing it.[2] Maurice believed what

Verdine lacked in maturity was exceeded by his enthusiasm and devotion to his craft (and brother). Retrospectively, Verdine told me his bass-playing style was not popular initially because it was different. The most obvious difference was his constant energetic onstage movement. In his words, "I am a performer who (as a bass player) sounds like a studio musician. I am a studio musician . . . as well as a performer. I was in the studio since I was 15-16 years old." During an audition for Warner Bros. Records, White performed shirtless in a leotard. Unlike most bassists, Verdine combined his bouncy performance with an uncanny ability to drive the band alongside the drummer. Immediately after joining EWF, all that mattered to Verdine was playing and performing the music. He credits his brother Maurice not for his concept per se but for giving him freedom to play the music.[3]

EWF signed with ex-football great turned actor Jim Brown's entertainment management company (Brown, Bloch and Covey) in part because of their shared belief that power was rooted in personal dignity. White admired Brown for both understanding creative processes and believing in what he (White) wanted to achieve. After RCA passed on signing EWF, they signed with Joe Smith of Warner Bros. and recorded a self-titled debut album produced by Joe Wissert that musically was progressive, diverse, and sonically raw. The debut's freewheeling jazzy arrangements, powerful horns, and heavy percussion displayed the band's Chicago roots. Released in February 1971, a *Rolling Stone* reviewer marked EWF's "heavy Sly influence" and "smooth harmonies" of the Fifth Dimension.[4] With the exception of Robert Christgau, critical reviews of the album were positive[5]

British critic Bruce Lindsay praised the debut album's social context and for reflecting the civil rights movement's themes of community and knowledge as positive alternatives to the despair of American society.[6]

EWF's maiden album appeared to accomplish White's goal to make music that had boundless energy, no parameters, and challenged listeners to examine their inner selves. However, the socially conscious critiques were antithetical to radio airplay and commercial success. For example, "Fan the Fire" is a throbbing mid-tempo tune with a message about the dying flames of love in an uncaring world where:

> Little children are starving in a foreign land
>     (Talk about it, brother)
> Man afraid to shake his brother's hand
>     (Fan the fire, fan the fire)
> Woman in trouble callin' but nobody cares
>     (Fan the fire, fan the fire)
> People denied the rights that are truly theirs
>     (It's a shame)

The album sold a modest 40,000 copies and reached No. 24 on the *Billboard* Top Soul Albums chart. One song, "Love Is Life" originally recorded by The Salty Peppers, reached No. 43 on the R&B charts. Despite these less-than robust numbers, Warner Bros. green-lit a second album.

Before recording the second album, an opportunity to perform the music for a Melvin Van Peebles film that offered a crude yet powerful inflammatory critique of White America and police brutality. White fails to note how the offer came to him, only that he easily agreed to do the music. One version suggests Van Peebles' ambitious young secretary allegedly actively sought a role in the film, only to refuse because of her boyfriend's (Maurice White) disapproval. In Mario Van Peebles' 2003 part-documentary/part-homage to his father, *Baadasssss*, Priscilla Watts, the secretary recommends her boyfriend Maurice White to do the film's music. Mario Van Peebles' film depicts White actively lobbying to do the music.[7]

According to the elder Van Peebles, since he lacked funding, he used good music as his film's selling point: "This had never been done before. Then everyone else copied."[8] The opening credits of *Sweet Sweetback's Baadasssss Song* listed "The Black community" as its stars and "Orchestra and Orchestrations" by then-unknown EWF. The band recorded the score while Van Peebles projected violent and sexual clips from the film. The result was a series of slippery funk and jazz loops in which Peebles can be heard chirping and screeching over. Van Peebles' limited budget compelled him to resist convention and release the soundtrack prior to the film's release as a promotional vehicle. The soundtrack also was sold in theater foyers. The strategy worked for Van Peebles because the film generated more than $10 million in its first few months and $15.2 million in total box office receipts.

Peebles scheme also worked for EWF because the Stax Records soundtrack, like the low-budget indie film, was commercially successful in its presentation of hymn-based vocalization and jazz rhythms. EWF got the publicity it desired although the themes in the film's score and images in the film were inconsistent with White's vision for EWF. The album reached No. 13 on the *Billboard* Top R&B Album chart.

The title selection, 7+ minutes of jazz riffs, earned surprisingly heavy radio airplay and paved the way for soundtracks like Isaac Hayes' *Shaft* (1971) and Curtis Mayfield's *Superfly* (1972). The film also facilitated Black filmmakers and artists with Afrocentric worldviews such as EWF.

Films such as *Sweetback* and other Black cultural products in the 1970s were important because the American government's successful infiltration of Black civil rights organizations stifled Black protest and eradicated militant Black leaders such as Eldridge Cleaver and H. Rap Brown. Black popular music and soul music in particular, were harder to silence as conduits for political expressions of the civil rights and Black Power movements. When *Sweetback* was released in March 1971, the Black Panther Party (BPP) was in disarray. There was a major split within the organization and many members left the party because of an opposition to a perceived diversion from revolution and self-defense. Huey Newton announced in 1971 that the BPP would adopt a nonviolent manifesto and focus on providing social services to Black communities. *Sweetback* could not save the BPP—by 1975 most of its activities had ended, and by 1982 the BPP was officially dissolved. EWF's direct impact on *Sweetback*'s success was minimal, but the film's impact on EWF was slightly more significant. Besides gaining much-needed publicity, EWF's future albums circumvented the posturing of Black male sexual prowess that signified much of Black popular cultural expressions in the immediate aftermath of *Sweetback*.

Black musicians such as Maurice White joined Black filmmakers and other creative artists in communicating the country's social and political conditions and serving as voices of Black communities. Yet White was cognizant of the cultural tensions at work. He understood how EWF's heavy percussive sounds, socially conscious messages, and even their Afrocentric dashikis and necklaces made out of bones startled some of the people he wanted his band to attract. White preferred to dress in jeans and a turtleneck—at least when he was not performing.

John Shaft's turtlenecks and trademark leather jackets from *Shaft* were accessories to his Black masculine sexual prowess persona crafted by the film's White creators. Although Shaft's Black tough guise was largely accepted by Black audiences, his sexualized masculinity, and misogyny also were inconsistent with Maurice White's idea of Black masculinity. He sensed that many Americans—Black and White—feared elements of this new Black consciousness they did not understand. Many questioned basketball superstar Lew Alcindor for changing his name to Kareem Abdul-Jabbar and were hostile toward Muhammed Ali after he joined the Nation of Islam. In the midst of these and other cultural tensions, White stayed true to his vision of positivity for EWF and developed messages more aligned with Black is Beautiful than Black Power.

One EWF performance exemplifies Black audiences' rejection of EWF's early sound. After Jim Brown booked EWF at LA's Maverick's Flat—also known as the Apollo of the West—the band was roundly booed which forced John Daniels, owner of the Crenshaw-area club, to turn out the lights on EWF. Daniels' blunt assessment of the performance was, "they weren't very good."[9] Black audiences did not appear ready for EWF's sound or appearance. Many older Black audience members preferred the clean-cut look and vocal harmonies of the doo-wop groups, or what Maurice frequently labeled as the drill-team approach. In the words of Warner Bros. promotion manager Perry "PJ" Jones, "We were, like, West Coast freaks."[10] Yet Jones saw White as someone who knew what he wanted and where he was going. But how would he get there?

White spent considerable time fine-tuning and outlining his concept to Jones (and anyone who would listen) because he desperately needed an ally inside Warner Bros. His concept was rooted in his belief that music was sacred and could lift people—who were already connected as humans—to higher places. His music would be without boundaries—his spiritual truth to uplift people and show them that "all spiritual paths, at their highest, have a unity." White believed he convinced Jones that his message would be embraced by everyone.[11] The question that remained for the timekeeper was whether or not he could convince his band to join him in his quest.

Near the end of 1971, Warner Bros. released EWF's second album, "The Need of Love" (*TNOL*). EWF continued to merge jazz, funk, and soul, but songs from *TNOL* were smoother and more polished than their debut album, and there were no elements of Black Power. This absence, alongside White's firm control of EWF's business and financial decisions created friction among some of the band members. Of the album's five songs, including a cover of Donny Hathaway's (1970) "Everything Is Everything," only "I Think about Lovin' You" was released as a single in February

1972 and received airplay on Black radio stations due to its more traditional R&B sound.[12]

Despite the single's success, written and sung by Sherry Scott, the album underperformed compared to EWF's debut album and inevitably contributed to the growing dissention among the band members. Some blamed Maurice White for EWF's lack of immediate success, while others failed to recognize him as the primary leader and fall in line with his way of thinking and doing. Although White apparently understood that leadership required accepting being challenged, he failed to effectively manage many of the personal and professional relationships within his band, which was a daunting task for a first-time band leader. Another point of view is that White was never going to get these older musicians to buy-in to his concept. White assumed (or hoped) that his band would accept his way of thinking as he did with Ramsey Lewis, or at least acquiesce. He also drew from his Chess Records experience to reject the decisions by committee approach. Both calculations proved costly.

Because Wade Flemons coveted the leadership role, his allegiance to White did not happen and he quit after White reminded him that he owned the band's name. Don Whitehead was next to depart and others would leave to form a new group (Colors). EWF's horn section moved on and shortly thereafter, guitarist Michael Beal, reducing EWF to the two White brothers. White conceded that he needed to improve his leadership style and provide more encouragement and inspiration to his team. He sought to rebuild the band with younger members who were talented and lacked the cynicism and coldhearted nature of the record business. White had little choice but to adhere to Mama's advice and Hill's laws to keep moving forward with a positive attitude. His next decisions demonstrated the necessity of patience and persistence to his concept.

EWF was one of a handful of Black artists on the Warner Bros. label. At the direction of Jim Brown, the label hired Denver native Perry "PJ" Jones as the first African American national promotion director for "special markets" (aka, "Black"). His initial work included promoting EWF's second album by making direct contact with Black radio air personalities and getting EWF product into record stores. Jones developed a new model by having EWF and other Black acts visit record stores (owned by Black DJs) to autograph albums for consumers. Jones shipped albums directly to DJs to sell in their stores and avoid payola practices. He also used more "traditional" methods like dispensing cocaine.[13] Despite Jones' efforts and his close partnership with White, Maurice remained dissatisfied with the label's support for EWF partly because of the lack of outreach to non-Black audiences. But his attention focused on recruiting younger musicians who would respect his leadership and buy into his concept.

After White informed Jones of the mass exodus of EWF band members, Jones reminded him of a group called Friends & Love who opened for EWF in Denver and recommended percussionist/vocalist Phillip Bailey who recently left Denver for Los Angeles to join a gospel group named the Stovall Sisters. After the group failed, Verdine White endorsed Bailey following a brief meeting without singing a single note. Bailey joined the auditions for additional members and suggested former Friends & Love keyboardist Larry Dunn. Dunn memorized the recordings from EWF's first two albums and played them during his successful audition.

The White brothers, Bailey and Dunn, continued to hold auditions. Before Michael Beal's departure, he suggested drummer Ralph Johnson who auditioned in December 1971 with only Verdine and Beal present. Since Verdine's bass was critical to any EWF drummer, his approval was good enough for Maurice. Johnson's addition pushed White from drums to the forefront on percussion and vocals, despite his hesitancy as a vocalist. After Johnson's hire, another endorsement led to guitarist Roland Bautista. Bautista, a rock-style guitar session player, was joined by saxophonist Ronnie Laws, the younger brother of jazz flutist Herbert Laws. EWF's revolving door swapped Helena Dixon briefly for vocalist Sherry Scott, but Dixon never appeared on any EWF album and quickly was replaced by former Friends of Distinction songstress Jessica Cleaves.

These personnel changes were not detrimental to the young band who rehearsed and toured at a frantic pace. As Verdine told me, "we just kept going, we were ready to flourish." Maurice White gave new band members creative freedom within his framework as he redirected some of his attention to the promotional support necessary for realization of his vision for EWF. As Phillip Bailey notes, EWF was definitely Maurice White's concept, although nobody at that time knew what the final vision would be. Larry Dunn is more emphatic—Maurice White had a vision, and he was going to stick to it.[14] The new band members worked hard to mesh their unique contributions and talents.

They respected Maurice's leadership as much as he embraced their youthfulness. In Bailey's words, the new lineup gave White "a burst of energy and inspiration in ways he never imagined or anticipated. We were open vessels, and Maurice melded our exuberance with his worldliness."[15]

Maurice's dream became a musical vision that he nurtured into a concept for EWF. He saw his dream as a calling that was tied to his faith, confidence, and self-love. For White, self-love is not only an important part of his faith but also the lack of self-love was "anti-God, dishonorable to his creation and a force of darkness."[16] White's belief about of self-love has merit given the verse from Matthew 22:37-40 (King James Version) in which the second commandment asks one to love thy neighbor as thyself. It makes sense to reiterate that White's concept called for a band that expressed how he felt about life, about God, and love. Self-love is a main theme of one of the two ballads on *TTWOTW*.

## Positivity and Self-Love

While most EWF songs embody in different ways Maurice White's doctrine of positivity, "All About Love" is a ballad more about positive thoughts than traditional love. Co-written by Maurice White and Larry Dunn, White dominates the vocals and Dunn directs the music. Verdine White jokingly told me it was EWF's first rap song because of brother Maurice's extended rapping. Lead vocalist Maurice White opens and closes the song with soliloquies addressed to listeners and not a lover. One of Maurice's positive claims is, "you are as beautiful as your thoughts, right on!". "All About Love" is as beautiful instrumentally as it is lyrically meandering. The 5+ minute ballad pontificates human aspirations such as the quest for autonomy and love. Many of the disjointed references to the heart, mind, and beauty could have ruined the lengthy song (sans closing interlude). Fortunately, the composition is salvaged by White's comforting lead vocals, extravagant orchestral arrangements, and angelic background vocals. The recording closes the album's first side (or track 4) and is sandwiched between Larry Dunn's Moog synthesizer interludes. Dunn also earns credit for the melody and flamboyant bridge chords accentuated by thunderous timpani rolls and brass riffs.

Immediately after Dunn's 18-second Moog interlude, the song opens with Dunn's piano chords underneath White's brief spoken intro informing listeners of the band's intent to let them know how they feel about love. The first two verses are dominated by Dunn's basic piano chords and White's tenor vocals. Strings replace Dunn's chords in the third verse paced by soft snare drum beats. White's last line of the third verse, "It's all about love, yeah" escorts the background vocals ("Ooooooh") as White sings the fourth verse. The instrumental bridge builds with brass and orchestration as the background vocals switch to a harmonized "Ahhhhhhhhhhh." White returns with a slightly softer melodic repeat of verses 3 and 4. His voice fills the sonic space again with light piano chords until he summons his lowest register to boldly proclaim, "Bound to fall in love one day. Surely and you need it. Pretty smile will always say "My dear," YEAH!". Dunn's piano, background vocals, and horns remain underneath White's lengthy closing soliloquy.

White's closing rap is more coherent than his beautifully sung but oblique lyrics. He reveals what he has admitted publicly—his desire for listeners to see EWF as extremely thoughtful and deep, when he brags: "We've studied all kinds of sciences and astrology and mysticism, world religion . . . they give you an insight to your inner self." His use of "we" reinforces EWF's message of universalism that encourages understanding of an inner self that promotes self-love. White's fascination with some of these subjects was not fully embraced by the other band members. Bailey admitted some members tried transcendental meditation, but his initial acceptance of White's universal spiritual views dissipated over time. As a Catholic, Bailey found mysticism creepy and was uneasy about the astrology embraced by Maurice and Verdine.[17]

Bailey could not refute White's next point about the duality of humans' spiritual and material (or hedonistic) sides: "Now, there's an outer self we got to deal with, you know? The one that likes to go to parties . . . that likes to dress up be cool, look pretty, all ego trips." White coolly delivers his primary message, "you gotta love you," which he follows by imploring, "if there ain't no beauty you got to make some beauty." Much of White's monologue is in step with certain tenets of the 1960s/1970s human potential movement and what morphed into new age philosophies. The song concludes with White's ad-libs which fade into Dunn's extended mini Moog interlude's cold ending.

## The Light

Light is an important concept to EWF. The term appears in several songs on *TTWOTW*: Lead vocalist Maurice White compels listeners in "All About Love" to "let the light shine all through your mind." The second verse of "Shining Star" reminds listeners the shining star comes into view "to shine its watchful light on you." "Yearnin' Learnin'" tells the story of the child born, "with a light to carry on." Fittingly, "See the Light" summons the spiritual forces of the universe to help "them [those in power] see the light." Although these references are figurative, it is worth noting that the main source of light on Earth is the sun while another supplier of light is fire. For EWF, light is the most universal and fundamental symbol of spirituality and divinity. Besides illumination, light is a source of knowledge, goodness and an avenger of evil and darkness in "See the Light."

The explicit spiritual theme in the lyrics of "See the Light" comes from co-writers Larry Dunn, Phillip Bailey, and Louise Anglin. Although little is known about Anglin, Dunn, and Bailey were raised as Catholics and perhaps the most outwardly religious members of the band. Larry Dunn composed the music and wrote half of the first verse sung by Bailey:

> *I'm a blossom, in the sun, sunshine of love,*
> *Singing loud to the one I love above.*

Phillip Bailey wrote the rest of the lyrics, Maurice produced it, and Charles Stepney's arrangements with the horns and strings made it the ideal rejoinder to the title track's sermon.

At its core, the 5:30 song is lead vocalist Bailey's prayer for individual salvation in a troubled world. His prayer of intercession solicits divine intervention for those in power until his "final song is sung."

The song's intense 35-second introduction begins in an unusual 7/8-time signature carried by Larry Dunn's mini Moog. The 7/8 time is a stamp on global music, fusion, and modern sound production techniques. The off-meter time of "See the Light" is also reminiscent of the African diasporic music from the likes of Santana. The up-tempo intro signifies human movement—not a foot race or rush to the alter but an inner pursuit in darkness for daylight. The protracted introduction is followed by medium tempo verses and jazzy instrumental bridges signifying an inner quest for tranquility conveyed seamlessly by harmonized falsettos:

> *Troubles everywhere, more than I can bear*
> *So I'm searching from within . . .*

Bailey's falsetto is matched by background vocals reminiscent of a chorus of angels. The prayer closes with the verse "Help them see the light" repeated six times in the midst of chord and octave changes and capped by Bailey's falsetto reaching the zenith of his four-octave register: "See The . . . Light!" This musical prayer is the only composition on *TTWOTW* that Maurice White does not share songwriting credits. Although White was raised by his grandmother in a Baptist church, he brought to EWF his own brand of universalism that rendered all faiths and philosophies equal. There would be religious conflicts between band members and Maurice, but not enough to stunt EWF's phenomenal growth in the aftermath of *TTWOTW*. The one sacred entity that all band members shared was music.

## Misunderstood Reasons

The other ballad on *TTWOTW*, "Reasons," like "All About Love," is not a traditional love song. EWF's albums before *TTWOTW* contained ballads such as "Keep Your Head to the Sky" and "Devotion" that were more about spirituality than romantic love. Although "Reasons" is neither spiritual or traditional love ballad, it is a beautifully composed song about sexual desire in a one-night stand.

"Reasons" is EWF's most well-known ballad despite band members' contention that many listeners misunderstand the song's central meaning. The recording garnered massive airplay on both R&B and pop stations despite never being released as a single. Bailey's suave falsetto provides a mesmerizing overlay to Stepney's lavish orchestral arrangement. The ballad's sheer musical splendor rendered it a love song played at weddings, which dumbfounded Bailey: "Didn't anyone bother to listen to the lyrics?"[18] It is conceivable that the powerful arrangement and Bailey's sensual vocals instigated listener indifference to the lust-driven lyrics. Unlike sex-laced recordings like Marvin Gaye's "You Sure Love to Ball," "Reasons" is a song about sex without sounding like one. To most, it sounds like a love song.

The composition stemmed from a Caribou conversation between Bailey and Maurice about the abundance of women available on the road. Bailey sings passionately about his vacillation turned guilt on a one-night stand. His sweet hums that open the song establish ownership of the song's message: "Now, I'm craving your body, is this real. Temperature's rising, I don't wanna feel, I'm in the wrong place to be real. Whoa and I'm longing to love you just for a night."

The chorus testifies the central dilemma and points to one of the keys to the song's widespread appeal. Listeners can identify with situations that provoke ambivalence about sexual desire. Bailey resonates this common sentiment in the chorus: "Reasons, the reasons that we're here. The reasons that we fear our feelings won't disappear." In the aftermath of passion, the disillusions surface: "And all our reasons start to fade." The background vocals' gentle serenade—"La La La La La La La La La"—bridges the harmonized duet between Bailey and the background vocals:

> . . . *All our reasons were a lie (all our reasons were a lie)*
> *After all our reasons love was left aside (love was left*
>     *aside)*

The 30-second instrumental bridge showcases Charles Stepney's lush symphonic arrangement of timpani/kettledrums, brass, and strings. Bailey re-sings the chorus to set up his climaxing (no pun intended) final verse. His last line delivers a heart-wrenching admonishment:

> *And, in the morning when I rise*
> *No longer feeling hypnotized . . .*
> *Had no pri-ii-ii-iide . . .*

The 5:00 recording closes with Bailey reiterating his failure to reconcile his illicit desire.

If *TTWOTW*'s studio version of "Reasons" enthralled listeners, the live versions—especially from *Gratitude*—left audiences awestruck. Bailey's croons, scats, and conversations with live audiences gave the song another dimension. One example is Bailey's call-and-response with saxophonist Don Myrick in which he applauds the soloist by asking, "He plays so beautiful, don't you agree?" Bailey's phrase was repeated in Black popular culture by such icons as Eddie Murphy (*Coming to America*) and Jay-Z.

EWF albums after *TTWOTW* contained more traditional love songs such as "Can't Hide Love" (*Gratitude*), "Imagination" (*Spirit*), "Love's Holiday," "I'll Write a Song for You," "Be Ever Wonderful" (*All N' All*), and "After the Love Has Gone" (*I Am*). All were very successful and provided additional weapons in their robust musical arsenal. In August 2021 EWF released "You Want My Love," a reinterpretation of "Can Hide Love" featuring singer-songwriter Lucky Daye and Kenneth "Babyface" Edmonds (producer, guitar). That same month, EWF performed the song at the rain-shortened "We Love NY" homecoming concert, produced by Clive Davis. Nearly fifty years after *TTWOTW*, EWF's legacy illuminates.

Themes such as self-love, mysticism, and even lust were not specific components of White's concept for EWF. However, they made their way into EWF's music catalog because they were messages listeners could relate to and/or reflected the experiences of EWF band members. Verdine White, Phillip Bailey and the other members of EWF were probably too young and inexperienced to fully appreciate Maurice's concept for EWF during their early years. Yet they shared his desire to be the best musicians they could be and were willing to follow his leadership in a united effort to make EWF great. Some even tried to adopt White's holistic lifestyle with varying degrees of success. The more time the band spent together they realized that being a successful ensemble of musicians required more than just individual musical expertise. It required a respect for leadership and willingness to cultivate collaboratively their creative talents. Maurice was committed to assembling and leading a creative team of musicians, even if it required more personnel changes— which it did. White's ability to overcome this leadership challenge required a more collaborative concept—a shared vision in rehearsals, the studio, on stage, and on the road.

# 4
# Presenting . . . Earth, Wind & Fire!

Perry Jones (and later Leonard Smith) often would appear center stage looking out to audiences in a theater or club—and later in pitch-black arenas, standing in a genie-like full-length glowing robe and turban with a sparkling diamond. In an omnipotent voice of a prophet, he proclaims, "Presenting! The Elements of the Universe, Earth! Wind! And Fire!"

The first time I saw EWF perform in person at the legendary Uptown Theater in Philadelphia, in March 1972, I had to settle for radio air personality Georgie Woods' introduction instead of Jones'. The Uptown, like Harlem's Apollo, was considered part of the chitlin' circuit, a string of theaters that the major soul revues would play to sometimes unforgiving audiences. Although I had attended many shows at the Uptown, I never saw any unruly treatment of performers by an audience. Perhaps because the performances were enjoyable.

The lineup included the New Birth and the Manhattans. Although I loved EWF's single "Think About Lovin You" from the airplay it received on Philly's WDAS, I knew nothing about EWF and had minimal expectations. Similarly,

I was not very familiar with the New Birth but enjoyed their cover of Perry Como's "It's Impossible" from their second (1971) album. EWF's performance got off to a strange start after WDAS' Woods' introduction to a rather sparse Sunday afternoon crowd. The band members sat silently on the stage floor in lotus positions as one by one members rose to play. Despite contrary accounts by White and Bailey, the audience reacted to EWF with an initial restlessness accompanied by sporadic hissing and murmuring. There was no booing nor do I recall any object being thrown onto the stage.[1]

I learned months later that the opening tune that caused the commotion was "Power." After the unusual beginning, the robust instrumental had the audience rocking. I could not help but notice the bandleader (center stage) playing an unrecognizable instrument in his hands. I heard its plucking sound periodically during "Power" and it sounded a bit eerie at first. But as an abortive drummer, I quickly became attracted to a sound that blended so nicely with rhythms. My impatient wait for the familiar ballad sung by the female vocalist on stage, "Think About Lovin You," was overcome by covers of ballads sung by a very young-looking falsetto named Phillip Bailey.

As a connoisseur of Philly soul music, I was drawn to Bailey's falsetto and wider vocal register compared to William "Poogie" Hart (Delfonics) or Russell Thompkins Jr. (Stylistics). He played congas and had some nice exchanges with the only female on stage. Bailey impressed me as the musician and vocalist I aspired (unrealistically) to be at that time in my life. I could not avoid my preoccupation with the tall, thin bass player who bounced up and down as if he was on a pogo stick.

His head-bobbing as he moved across the stage with ease. From a pure musical standpoint, I preferred the saxophone solo over his bass solo. But what stood out the most to me was EWF's spirited stage presence bore no resemblance to the choreographed steps and matching outfits of the soul groups I had grown accustomed to seeing at the Uptown. My only clear recollections of the New Birth were its slightly larger number of band members and performance that was less musically proficient (compared to EWF). EWF was in constant motion compared to the stagnant New Birth. I had no remembrances of the Manhattans and enjoyed EWF more than the New Birth.

EWF had a unique, inimitable sound and an onstage dynamism that I had never observed from musicians. I sensed the audience also appreciated musicians who defied the uniformity in presentation of most Uptown performers. After the show, I walked down Broad Street to the subway knowing I heard something fresh and feeling I discovered something worthy of further exploration. Unbeknownst to me at the time, EWF had a similar reaction to my own in their downtown Philadelphia hotel as Phillip Bailey expresses: "We sensed something unique and very special had just happened that we needed to affirm together . . . we were strong about the Concept."[2] I bought EWF's *TNOL* album and ascertained the electric kalimba as the bandleader's unknown hand instrument. I was confused after comparing the photographs of band members on *TNOL* with the EWF I saw at the Uptown. My confusion dissipated several months later upon comparing photos of the EWF on their latest album, *Last Days and Time* (*LDAT*) to those on *TNOL*. I realized there had been personnel changes after their second album but did not know there was a debut album. I was less concerned by the band's membership because I loved their sound—especially the songs on *LDAT*, which EWF featured at the Uptown. It took some time and effort, but I eventually found EWF's debut album on Warner Bros.

White's dissatisfaction with Warner Bros.' promotional support for EWF was compounded by learning from Perry Jones about racist remarks made by a Warner Bros. sales director. White asked Jim Brown to release EWF from its management contract and after a series of meetings, Brown agreed with White's preference for an East coast label that promoted the band to a broader audience. Brown's only condition was that White hire BBC's Leonard Smith as EWF's tour manager. Smith would remain tour manager until 1985 and after Perry Jones' departure from Warner Bros., was best known publicly for his rousing onstage introductions: "Presenting the elements—Earth! . . . Wind! . . . and Fire!"[3]

Bob Cavallo replaced Jim Brown as manager and marshaled a deal with Clive Davis at Columbia Records. After a secret audition in Los Angeles and as an opening act for John Sebastian in New York, Davis was blown away by the new version of EWF and signed the group along with their first Columbia album for about $100,000.[4] EWF's six newest members joined the White brothers in recording an album very distinct from the two previous Warner Bros. releases. EWF began recording *LDAT* in April 1972 and White's goal was to broaden both the band's musical foundation and followers. One strategy to accomplish this was to follow a music business tradition to record songs that had been hits with other artists. According to White, the recommendation came from Clive Davis.

White's experiences with Chess, Capitol, and Warner Bros. led to a distrust of the hype from corporate executives. Yet he needed support from Clive Davis, who was hired largely to build Columbia's popular (and Black) music portfolio. White contends he was oblivious to EWF's placement in Columbia's Special Markets Division. His apparent indifference to corporate sentiments would prove useful as entertainment conglomerates annexed Black popular music and other cultural expressions.[5] White also was cognizant of the ways segregation and racism in the record industry held back EWF and other Black recording artists.

It was Phillip Bailey's idea for EWF to perform covers of Bread's "Make It with You" and Pete Seeger's "Where Have All the Flowers Gone?" on tours since he sang both with Friends & Love.[6] EWF recorded both songs for *LDAT* which appears consistent with White's desire for the Columbia album debut to discard messages of Black Power or male sexual gallantry. He also aspired to pay homage to Marvin Gaye's "What's Going On," a 1971 game-changer for Black music in its critique of America's social climate and the Vietnam War. "What's Going On" was more than Gaye's crowning artistic achievement; it opened up other Black artists such as EWF to new creative possibilities. Later in 1971, Isaac Hayes dropped "Black Moses" and Sly and the Family Stone released "There's a Riot Goin' On,"—presumed responses to "What's Going On." By 1972, Gaye's Motown labelmate Stevie Wonder would follow Gaye's lead and take creative control of his career with "Talking Book." Gaye's concept album also paved the way for Wonder's "Songs in the Key of Life" until the era of concept recordings ended in the mid-1970s.

Although Gaye's album forged a path for EWF to merge genres and combine sacred and profane messages, *LDAT* obviously did not achieve anything close to the impact of Gaye's classic. Although some critics praised EWF's fresh fusion sound, *LDAT* earned mixed critical reviews and spawned no hit songs. The October 1972 release rose to No. 15 on Billboard's Top Soul Albums. Besides the 8-minute instrumental "Power" discussed earlier, another song worth noting is "Mom," which reached No. 39 on the Cashbox Top R&B singles chart. Lastly, "I'd Rather Have You," a ballad written by songwriter Skip Scarborough, represented White's willingness to expand his creative team through collaboration. Calling it "the most mature song" EWF had recorded to that point, "I'd Rather Have You," highlighted Jessica Cleaves' rich alto lead vocals that previously were only heard on the Friends of Distinction's "I'd Really Hope You Do."[7] The song also illustrates Cleaves' range that would be heard on EWF's next album. The unheralded, yet beautiful "I'd Rather Have You" has background vocals accentuated by "ba-da-pa-da-ba-da-ya," which became a lyrical vocalized staple of EWF.

The new EWF labored to make its mark via live performances at clubs, colleges, theaters, and some of the larger new arenas that were being constructed on the East coast. If the band was not touring, it was rehearsing and the rehearsals were grueling. There were fewer distractions in LA because EWF was not as well-known on the West coast as the East coast where they had more live performances and local television appearances. The band discovered college audiences to be loyal, Black audiences tough, and that some club owners refused to pay the band after performances. When shows were canceled at the last minute, White tried to deliver the bad news to his young band members as encouragingly as possible. He was convinced of his observation dating back to his Ramsey Lewis days that "a different generation with different needs was hungry for a different music."[8] This new generation of Black club and college audiences became EWF's core audience, something White never forgot.

In fact, the young members of EWF felt college audiences related to the band's youthfulness, and Bailey echoed White's view that they "were looking for something fresh."[9] EWF's predominantly Black East coast audiences seemed particularly tuned in to their performances. A mutual appreciation was mounting between EWF and their audiences that is captured both on *TTWOTW*'s recording "Happy Feelin'" and in a scene from the *TTWOTW* motion picture. EWF's emphasis on (and enjoyment of) live performances during their early days is on full display in the funky fun-loving "Happy Feelin'."

## Happy Feelin'

The 8-minute scene is one of the film's rare highlights and presents EWF on stage at a New Jersey roller skating rink performing "Happy Feelin'" live as the joyous Black skaters circle the rink. The song creates a communal experience through a connection of EWF's joy in creating and sharing music to listeners' pleasurable responses. The cheery composition is one outcome of Maurice White encouraging band members to write collaboratively. "Happy Feelin'," co-written by Maurice White, Phillip Bailey, Verdine White, Larry Dunn, and Al McKay, is both primal and complex in its instrumentalizations. The 3:15 up-tempo jam is driven by Ralph Johnson's snappy drums and Verdine's running bass line. EWF did not miss a beat when rhythm guitarist Al McKay and saxophonist Andrew Woolfolk replaced Roland Bautista and Ronnie Laws respectively after the *LDAT* album. "Happy Feelin'" gets much of its zest from Woolfolk's tenor sax octave-jump melodies, and blissful touches from White's kalimba. The high-energy song kicks off with 10 seconds of snare, bass, and conga drums in a standard time signature of four beats per bar. Larry Dunn's Fender chords keep pace as Woolfolk's sax riffs set up the first verse. The falsetto vocals by Maurice and Phillip express their joy of sharing music whose reception evokes powerful sensations:

*Feelin', happy feelin'*
*In the music that we're givin'*

The groove gets even funkier when Woolfolk's tenor sax and White's kalimba enter the foreground during the extended instrumental bridge. The second verse unites a message of sharing and caring with EWF's songwriting practice of ensuring the lyrics yield to the groove:

*Share the feelin' with your brother*
*Don't stop carin' for one another*

The verse continues with EWF's basic rationale for happily sharing their music—unspecified life conditions warrant a longing for pleasure:

> *There's a reason, that we're pleasin'*
> *What you're yearnin', life's a burnin*

The second instrumental break and bridge lead to a high-pitched crescendo as the falsettos climb the scales under Bailey's vocal vamps. The refrain, "Feelin', Happy Feelin', Happy Feelin'," is repeated three times followed by Maurice White's snappy tenor vocal breakdown: "Feel, feel feel what you wanna' feel, feel feel" (repeated). The song closes by White repeating "feel" "feel" and "yeah yeah, yeah," with kalimba, and sax rifts. "Happy Feelin'" expresses EWF's desire for people to join them in letting go of restrictions and feeling good with their music. The song is bound to make listeners feel good, dance, sing, and even merrily roller skate.

In addition to the film's live version of "Happy Feelin'," *TTWOTW*'s studio version closes the film during credits with footage from an EWF concert. The concert footage displays Verdine playing airborne and Dunn and his keyboards spinning upside down in mid-air—two of the many highlights of EWF live performances during the 1970s.

## Fire Shows

EWF took a page from Napoleon Hill's *Law of Success* by not telling people what they can do but showing them instead. *LDAT*'s lukewarm record sales and lack of hit songs validated

Maurice White's contention that EWF needed to allocate more time to rehearsing and performing than recording. His strategic decision to focus on performing accomplished three related objectives: (1) to build a core audience, comprised mostly of African Americans; (2) to broaden the band's audience base by performing at diverse venues for non-Black audiences; and (3) to use the revenues from live performances to keep the band solvent and invest any additional revenues from constant touring in superior equipment for future (and larger) live performances.

The latter two objectives were accomplished by a July 1972 EWF performance in London at a confab of CBS label executives, sales departments, promotional directors, and A&R divisions. The international venue grave EWF an opportunity to expand its audience base by performing to a new and unique audience. Although Clive Davis grappled with the costs of showcasing his new signees at the event, he wanted to prove that his Philadelphia International Records (PIR) deal was the beginning of Columbia's successful commitment to Black music. He reasoned that EWF's diverse musical portfolio would illustrate the links between the jazz fusion of (CBS artists) Miles Davis and Herbie Hancock and Philadelphia International Record's R&B crossover hits. Although CBS used the event to showcase new and upcoming artists, EWF's uniqueness made Davis nervous.[10]

Going into the show, Azteca, a Latin rock spin-off band fronted by ex-Santana members Pete and Coke Escovedo, was hailed as the next big thing. EWF not only out-performed the band but also followed White's lead, their clean-living approach stood in stark contrast to Azteca's excessive drinking and partying.[11] Before an audience that included George Harrison and Ringo Starr, EWF's clearheaded performance proved worthy of Clive Davis' introduction (over the low rumble of kalimba's intro to "Power"): "This group is going to be around for a very long time, and they are going to make history.[12] EWF gave a triumphant performance that amazed CBS executives from all over the world and gave Davis a shivering "all-time thrill."[13] Following the buzz generated from the CBS convention, a prophetic Davis consented to White's request for an equipment upgrade.

When Ronnie Laws left EWF to join Hugh Masekela, Philip Bailey recommended Denver native and saxophonist Andrew Woolfolk. Shortly after Laws' exit, guitarist Roland Bautista followed suit and was replaced by Al McKay. White let McKay go after a few months for missing a gig (due to his prior commitments to Stax Records) and was replaced by Johnny Graham (who played briefly with the New Birth). White knew that to keep a band together, increasing revenues were essential. A band earned more money with high-paying gigs, and to warrant high-paying gigs, hit recordings, and big-time live performances were essential. Although EWF lacked hit songs, it was demonstrating a unique performative prowess that helped broaden its audience. For example, the additions of Andrew Woolfolk and Johnny Graham gave the band's concert performances even more creative energy.[14] The new EWF had been together for half a year and were outperforming the other groups on the concert lineups. Until the hit-recording drought came to an end with their next album, EWF continued to tour and refine their live performances.

Another EWF performance is noteworthy for achieving White's objective to build its Black audience base. EWF's first national televised presentation was on *Soul!*, a pioneering performance arts program produced by New York public television WNDT/WNET marked White's connection to the burgeoning Black arts movement. More importantly, as the only nationally televised program dedicated to Black cultural expression, *Soul!* provided EWF with a unique platform that was distinct from the concert, theater, and club performances that were driving the band's modest ascension. Unlike EWF's London performance in which it shared the stage with such acts as Loggins and Messina, Andy Williams, and Maynard Ferguson's big band, being the featured guest on *Soul!* bolstered its commitment to Black audiences.

*Soul!* aired from 1968 to 1973 and showcased Black musicians from a variety of genres as well as writers, dancers, politicians, and social activists. *Soul*'s notable guests included James Baldwin, Nikki Giovanni, Donny Hathaway, Stevie Wonder, Amiri Baraka, Sidney Poitier, and Harry Belafonte. A 1969 Harris Poll estimated that more than 65 percent of African American New York City households with access to the series viewed *Soul!* on a regular basis.[15] The series promoted African American artistry and culture, but not in the least common denominator way of commercial television. The performance followed the October 1972 release of *LDAT* which gave the new EWF members a chance to showcase their first professional album. As I watched the video of EWF performance on *Soul!* (many years later), I felt as though they were relaxed and in unison with the Black community—a construct preferred over audience by *Soul!* creator, producer and host Ellis B. Haizlip. EWF was not playing for an audience, they were sharing their music with *their* community.

EWF's 32-minute performance on *Soul!* was recorded in December 1972 before a live intimate studio audience and aired early January 1973. The episode began with a close-up of Maurice White's hands strumming his kalimba under the announcer's introduction to the episode titled "Elements." White's kalimba continues in the background as each of the eight members are introduced. The extended introduction to "Power" continues with the kalimba returning to the foreground as Bailey plays the congas and other members add various percussion instruments in a similar fashion to their Uptown concert. The audience mildly grooved to the beat anticipating the musical eruption they were about to partake. The 6-minute instrumental "Power" was followed by Phillip Bailey's soul-stirring cover of James Taylor's "Don't Let Me Be Lonely Tonight." The third song was an instrumental that featured a shirtless rail-thin Verdine White solo while his bass laid flat on the stage floor. The televised set closed with two songs from *LDAT*, "Mom" and "Time is on Your Side."

The studio audience's fervent response to EWF comprised a zealous engagement that included dancing with band members. For brief seconds, some in the audience appeared stunned—as if they had never seen a band perform in this manner, but their head nods of approval signaled appreciation for EWF's musical performance. Many in the audience reminded me of those at the Uptown Theater who were not only witnessing something surprisingly different but also participating in something remarkably special.

Haizlip sought to represent Black music as a conversation between musicians and audiences. His goal was for the audience to appear "in relationship to a performance that [they are] enjoying as opposed to a performance that is being presented for [them]."[16] EWF was the ideal band to fulfill his goal.

Maurice White compared the performance on *Soul!* to subsequent EWF television appearances by saying it was more "organic, more distinctive and quirky—more of who EWF really was."[17] *Soul!* facilitated a natural bond between EWF and viewers in part because the performance remained true to the show's refusal to divide Black arts into high vs. low culture, bestowing a communal experience. EWF was hailed by the *Soul!* audience because of the band's mesmerizing connection to audiences similar to their performances for college students, many of them at Historically Black College and Universities (HBCUs).

When EWF resumed travel on the eastern seaboard in rented station wagons, Al McKay returned as a second guitarist at White's request. The New Orleans native's first professional gig was with the Ike & Tina Turner Revue before becoming a member of The Watts 103rd Street Rhythm Band. The funk guitarist McKay formed a pairing with Johnny Graham's hot blues guitar that delivered one of the many EWF musical signatures—complimentary lead and rhythm guitars. After recording their fourth album, *Head to the Sky* (*HTTS*) in April 1973, EWF's station wagon tours continued at a frantic pace throughout the year. The young musicians felt capable of enduring the rigors of extended road trips. However, when Phillip Bailey was called a "nigger" for the first time when the band got lost in New Jersey, he chalked it up as a rare "dues-paying" experience that their predecessors had to endure on a regular basis on the chitlin' circuit.[18]

Racial hostilities and experiences such as last-minute cancellations forced EWF to confront the dual realities of both America's social environment and its music industry. Although Maurice White's worldliness and street-savvy offered some measure of support, he tended to isolate himself on the road and used the time to study and refine his concept. At one point on the road, the entire band followed his lead by becoming vegetarian, but that did not last long. White was compelled to evolve as a bandleader. He was beginning to realize that he was responsible to both himself and his band. White became more collaborative in rehearsals and the studio. He encouraged bandmates to write and worked as closely with Bailey on the vocal arrangements as he did with Larry Dunn on the music. White's determination to succeed would not be at the expense of his philosophical or spiritual principles. *HTTS,* released in June 1973, provided evidence that White's improving leadership was paying off.

## Finally, a Hit!

*HTTS* was EWF's first gold album peaking at No. 2 on the *Billboard* Top Soul Albums and twenty-seventh on the *Billboard* 200. *HTTS* showcased Larry Dunn's multifaceted keyboard skills on organ, clavinet, and Fender Rhodes. The album's jazz-funk was in line with the era's Black music turned out by Roy Ayers and Lonnie Liston Smith, The Latin influences in songs like "Evil," "Clover," and the lengthy version of Edu Lôbo's instrumental "Zanzibar" signified EWF's embrace of jazz and world music. *HTTS*'s intersection of Black, African, and Latin music deconstructed essentialist notions of Black music.

The band's first hit single, "Evil," co-written by Maurice White and Phillip Bailey (Bailey's first songwriting credit), made stellar use of the duo guitars of Al McKay and Johnny Graham, the layered vocals of White and Bailey, and zesty runs by White's kalimba. From the opening track's attention-grabbing thunderclap, Dunn's Fender Rhodes jump starts "Evil" and remains dominant throughout the melody of the 5:12 recording. Lyrically, "Evil" points to the duality of humans while rendering a restrained, yet sobering and sympathetic message about race in America:

> *Beauty in our face you see, tryin' to hide all our misery . . .*
> *But evil, runnin' through my brain, me and evil are about*
>     *the same.*

The most successful single on *HTTS*, "Keep Your Head to the Sky," provides a positive spiritual message while pleasantly daring in combining two oppositional Black musical traditions—secular jazz and blues with the sacred Black church and gospel music. The velvety ballad written by Maurice White (released as a single in October 1973) reached No. 23 on the *Billboard* Hot Soul Songs chart. White imbued the song with his own quest for a musical purpose and spiritual awakening. His uplifting composition posits a grounding in individual faith. Bailey recalls when White brought the song to him, it brought tears to his eyes.[19] The song's spiritual dimensions are as clear as Bailey's silky falsetto:

*Master told me one day, I'd find peace in every way,*
*but in search for the clue, wrong things I was bound to do.*
*Keep my head to the sky, for the clouds to tell me why,*
*As I grew with strength, Master kept me as I repent.*

As the song nears conclusion with harmonized tenor background vocals yielding to Bailey's rising lead falsetto, the instrumentation ends followed by three harmonized "Keep Your Head to the Sky." On the third, we hear Bailey and Cleaves ascending higher in a whistle-like register. In popular music at that time only Minnie Riperton could hit these high notes. Bailey—a huge admirer of Riperton—seemed to join Cleaves to see how high they could sing the final line. It survived the final mix as a piercing cold punctuated the message of affirmation and optimism. White's memoir expresses how the song

gave hope to young African Americans.
I wanted the Black men of Earth,
Wind and Fire to inspire self-worthiness.
I wanted to show confidence in our own heritage . . .
We wanted our Black fans to stand tall
and fulfill their highest potential from a
position of cultural strength.[20]

The cover of *HTTS* depicts EWF's male members shirtless on a white background surrounded by multicolored flowers.

Jessica Cleaves is centered in a white full-length dress and turban head-wrap. Cleaves' arms are spread downward in a protective manner with one hand grasping Verdine White's right hand and the other clutching Andrew Woolfolk's left hand. Verdine's left hand and Woolfolk's right hand are on Cleaves' waist as the three are the only ones standing. The other band members are seated, kneeling, or lying prone and surrounded by flowers as Maurice clutches his own floral bouquet. The cover corresponds to the love and peace movement of the 1970s that some saw as antithetical to Black America and certainly the Black Power movement that White eschewed. The photographic presentation fulfilled White's desire for EWF to personify a new form of Black masculinity that was sensitive, nurturing, and vulnerable. Despite Jessica Cleaves' limited role in the music, her center position on the album's cover signified EWF's acceptance of Black femininity. Unfortunately, Cleaves chose to exit EWF's revolving door (she later joined George Clinton's Parliament) as the band's last female vocalist.

Undeterred by another personnel change, the band members were immersed in making EWF successful. When they were not rehearsing, performing, or recording, members found time to jam informally. These jam sessions worked to strengthen their comradery and musical cohesion.

The commercial success of *HTTS* lifted EWF to the opening act in large arenas for the likes of B.B. King, Gladys Knight, and the Pips, War, and Parliament-Funkadelic. EWF performed for audiences they described as Black, White, young, and hip. One notable occasion was a Madison Square Garden opening in which EWF demolished a diminished

Sly & the Family Stone. From road manager Leonard Smith's commanding introduction to Verdine White playing in mid-air (using Mary Martin's *Peter Pan* harness), EWF gave audiences one performative jolt after another. Even EWF concerts in large venues were becoming communal events in which the band joined their audiences in affirmations of their collective social and spiritual aspirations. The band was establishing a symbiotic relationship between their live concert performances and studio recordings. In so doing, EWF broadened conceptions of Black music and its audiences.

## Black Music

Maurice White did not consciously set out to change Black music, opting instead to produce music that would alter the lens through which it was viewed. White expanded the boundaries of Black music while remaining faithful to the Black audiences who helped propel his band to international acclaim. EWF's ability to broaden Black popular expression was incumbent on its musical and performative capacities to embody the symbolic and material values of Black music in both historical and contemporary manifestations. I find musical evidence in songs from EWF's four Columbia albums such as a rendition of an African American spiritual ("Open Our Eyes"), jazz recordings such as "Spasmodic Movements," blues ("Tee Nine Chee Bit"), soul ("Reasons" and "All About Love"), funk ("Mighty Mighty" and "Shining Star"), Latin ("Zanzibar" and "Caribou"), and Brazilian music ("Brazilian Rhyme"). Although EWF did not compose traditional African music, some of their songs and musical interludes incorporated elements of African music ("Drum Song" and "Africano"). Performatively, the kalimba, congas, other drums, and percussion, call-and-response verses, Afrocentric wardrobes, and on-stage dance promulgated symbolic and material values of Blackness. Collectively, they encapsulated contemporary and historical Black music ideals. To their credit, EWF avoided essentialist narratives of Blackness and patriarchal tropes of Black masculinity and male sexual prowess often found in Black music.

White and Columbia Records succeeded in expanding the band's Black American audience base in ways an African American record label like Motown or Stax seemed unable or unwilling to do. In fact, chief among the reasons White did not contract with a Black label was to give him the creative autonomy to create an amalgam of Black music styles for the world to enjoy and find meaning. The Columbia Records corporate infrastructure's push for crossover success paved the way for EWF to execute White's concept to produce new styles of music that everybody could enjoy.

In 1970, the "Big Six" major labels consisted of CBS Records, Warner Bros., RCA, Capitol-EMI, Polygram, and MCA. Under the leadership of Clive Davis, the CBS conglomerate became the most successful music industry entity to produce, distribute, and market Black popular music. In late 1971, Logan Westbrooks, a Black pioneer in the music industry, came to CBS as the first director of Special Markets (their newly created Black music division).[21]

CBS Records consisted of Columbia Records—the label to which Clive Davis signed EWF, Epic Records, and a group of associated labels. One of those associated labels was Philadelphia International Records (PIR), the brainchild of "Philly" sound progenitors Kenneth Gamble, Leon Huff, and Thom Bell. Gamble and Huff signed a deal with CBS Records in 1971 to produce and distribute music from Harold Melvin and the Blue Notes, Billy Paul, and the O'Jays. In 1973, T-Neck Records inked a distribution agreement with CBS Records for the Isley Brothers.[22]

In an effort to better understand Black music, CBS Records commissioned the Harvard University Business School to conduct a scientific study. Westbrooks served as the coordinator of the study titled, "A Study of the Soul Music Environment Prepared for Columbia Records Group." The Harvard team was officially titled the "Columbia Records Project Group." According to Westbrooks, the study's rationales included determining CBS's profit potential and the crossover potential of Black artists. When the study was conducted in 1972, CBS Records had only two acts they felt could effectively penetrate the Black market: Sly Stone and Santana. Among the study's chief recommendations were to purchase already developed talent rosters from companies like Philadelphia International Records, revive and re-establish proven talents (Isley Brothers and the O'Jays), and develop upcoming groups such as EWF and Harold Melvin and the Blue Notes.[23]

White's major takeaway from the Harvard study was that major labels were instructed to buy their way into Black music. He cited his good friend David Porter (a Stax insider) among the many in the industry who regarded Columbia's distribution deal with Stax as a disaster.[24] On the other hand, one direct outcome of the study was Westbrooks' creation of CBS' Black Music Marketing division (BMM) in 1973. BMM was headed by Black music marketing pioneer, LaBaron Taylor. Although other labels copied this approach and hired Black executives for most of the decade, it caused some initial tensions between EWF and Columbia.

When EWF moved from Warner Bros. to Columbia Records in 1972, the band was assigned to CBS' Special Markets. After the creation of BMM, there were continuing clashes between pop and Black promotion executives when a Black act like EWF crossed over from Black radio to top-forty radio. According to one CBS/BMM executive, Maurice White was adamant that EWF music be handled by pop promoters. Unlike most Black artists at CBS, EWF was assigned to a White product manager, although band members maintained their ties to BMM staff. Ultimately, the success of EWF, PIR, and the Isley Brothers provided BMM with a forumula for success.[25] White understood his goal to broaden EWF's appeal was futile without resonating with Black audiences.

Even the news in June 1973 that Clive Davis had been fired as president of CBS Records did not curtail EWF's methodical rise. Like the flowers that engulfed them on the cover of *HTTS*, EWF was in full bloom. Buoyed by the success of *HTTS* and their live concerts, a self-assured EWF went to Colorado's Caribou Ranch to record their fifth studio album, *Open Our Eyes* (*OOE*). Verdine White was thrilled with the opportunity to record at the same venue used by Elton John and other musicians. For him, the isolation allowed the band to "stretch out" and achieve their shared goals. As Maurice White moved closer to constructing a creative team to achieve his vision and execute his concept, he used Caribou's secluded setting to abandon his isolation from band members. His leadership adjustments seemed to be working, yet he also was motivated by apprehension of the impact success might have on his band members—and perhaps himself.

White brought his younger brother Fred from EWF's touring group as the band's second drummer. Fred White started with Donny Hathaway at the age of sixteen before he joined Little Feat. The elder White's move raised some eyebrows inside the band. However, since Maurice played many of the drum parts himself in the studio, hiring Fred lessened that load so he could focus more on collaborative composing and singing. Maurice also believed EWF needed a more consistent and sustained groove and Fred provided a solid pocket and relied less on fills. As EWF's co-lead vocalist, Phillip Bailey's role in the band's success was obvious. He thought Maurice's idea of combining drummers was a great idea. As a percussionist, he easily made the transition to singing and playing (congas) with two drummers. Because Bailey knew that adding his congas to the blend did not matter until the groove is locked down, he anticipated how drummers White and Johnson would complement each other allowing his percussion to be "icing on the cake."[26] The two drummers also injected more elements of funk at the expense of jazz in *TTWOTW*.

EWF's fifth studio album, *OOE*, is a triumphant homage blending Black, African, and Latin music traditions and EWF's first commercially successful album to generate a top hit in "Mighty Mighty," which was released as the first single one month before the album's March 1974 release. The recording caused a bit of a hullabaloo among some White radio programmers and music industry executives. The song's self-empowerment theme functioned in the tradition of Black music to uplift and empower Black people by instilling self-dignity and racial pride. Written by Maurice and Verdine White, "Mighty Mighty" evinced many of the signature components of EWF's sound such as stacked vocals of Phillip Bailey and Maurice White, the heavy funk chords of Al McKay, brawny horn countermelodies, and Johnny Graham's blues guitar. Because of the era's racial dynamics and the record industry's proclivity to stifle the creative impulses of Black musicians, the song's chorus apparently generated some controversy: "We are people, of the mighty, mighty people of the sun."

People of African descent have been called "sun people" or "people of the sun" because of their melanin and African habitats are areas where the sun shines brightest. Because Maurice White believed that racism's legacy in the United States left many Black people confused, he wanted "Mighty Mighty" to instill racial pride. Larry Dunn recalls Maurice White telling him about pop radio stations refusing to play the song because of alleged "racist" lyrics. White's response to Dunn was the last time he checked, the sun shined on everybody.[27] "Mighty Mighty" instilled a sense of Black pride that was uncomfortable to some Whites such as EWF's manager Bob Cavallo. Although "Mighty Mighty" topped the soul charts at No. 4, Cavallo told White the recording would have been bigger without the "Black Power" message.[28] Cavallo and those who condemned the lyrics as racist conflated Black Power with self-empowerment and ignored other verses in "Mighty Mighty" as "spread ya love for a brighter day," and the chorus', "in our hearts lie all the answers, to the truth you can't run from." Some people *can* run from the truth, sun people don't have that privilege.

"Mighty Mighty" is an important song because of its universal message of overcoming obstacles with confidence and determination. White believed the message was important for everyone, especially African Americans because of racism's pervasiveness. The themes of empowerment through edification and morality in "Mighty Mighty" continued in songs from *TTWOTW* such as "Yearnin' Learnin'," "All About Love," and "Shining Star".

### "*You want to be treated like a rock band . . .*

. . . well, here ya go, pal."[29] Those were Cavallo's words to Maurice White prior to EWF's August 1973 tour in Bangor, Maine's 6,500-seat auditorium as an opening act for hard rock band Uriah Heep. However, when White told Cavallo back in 1972 he wanted EWF to be treated like a rock act, he aspired for Columbia Records to provide EWF equitable marketing and promotion opportunities. As a student of the music industry, White was mindful of its recent growth and how several rock bands grew from small-time operations into huge money-making machines due largely to large concert performances and the White audiences they attracted. Audiences in these large venues expected theatrics in addition to music and White was eager to oblige. Americans were spending $2 billion a year on music, which was $700 million more than the whole movie industry grossed from ticket sales in one year and about three times the amount of money taken in by all spectator sports.[30] In response to these industry trends, EWF developed stage performances that outshined most bands, Black or White.

ZZ Top joined EWF and Uriah Heep on the tour and reportedly in every show, EWF was the favorite of the predominantly White audiences. Despite Uriah Heep being at its peak in 1973, repeated calls for EWF encores led to EWF being removed from the tour. Although EWF's last appearance with Uriah Heep was October 1, the publicity and popularity that EWF earned from the abbreviated tour led to additional bookings and increased name recognition.[31]

I discovered several fan posts on YouTube complimenting EWF's performance on the Uriah Heap tour: "In 1973 I went to see Uriah Heep and the show was opened by the unknown Earth Wind & Fire. They were awesome and blew us white kid rock fans away. The next day I bought my first E,W & F album. I've remained a fan all my life." Another post touted EWF's showmanship: "EWF blew the roof off the coliseum. At one point, Verdine jumped down into the crowd and danced his way through it as he played. He eventually ended up dancing with a woman . . . even giving her a looooong kiss-all without missing a beat. They were as much fun to watch as they were to listen to." Interestingly, these posts appeared with video from EWF's television appearance on *Soul!*.

Before the March 1974 release of *OOE* (and after the February release of "Mighty Mighty"), Cavallo brought another seemingly peculiar booking to Maurice White.

California Jam was a rock music festival held at the Ontario Motor Speedway that Cavallo foresaw as a pathway to the broader audience EWF was building. Yet an outdoor rock concert in the Woodstock vein appeared at odds with EWF's dedication to higher consciousness and no drug/healthy lifestyle. To some, EWF lacked appeal to the vast majority who traditionally attended Woodstock-type concerts. White understood that every decision he made impacted the band's promising career and concluded the event could augment EWF's expanding audience. Because EWF had opened for Rod Stewart, Uriah Heep, and other big names, White was confident that his young musicians could handle the novelty and magnitude of California Jam. He was correct in his assessment of his band, but any questions regarding the audience response at California Jam might be found in EWF's White college student following as well as their endearing fans from their tours with rock bands.

White also evidently considered the event in a larger sociocultural context. He envisioned a White America that was becoming more accepting of Black people as White majorities had elected Tom Bradley mayor of EWF's Los Angeles home. As the only Black act on the lineup, EWF stayed true to themselves and performed four original songs and no covers. EWF appeared second among the eight bands under a warm sun before 200,000+ people at one of the era's last large rock festivals. EWF followed Rare Earth—a White Motown rock band that earned Black radio airplay. After EWF came the Eagles with Jackson Browne, Seals and Croft, Black Oak Arkansas, Black Sabbath, Deep Purple, and Emerson, Lake, and Palmer. EWF's set included a Verdine

White bass solo that appeared to drive many in the audience into a frenzy.

A *New York Times* review described the April concert lineup as "good, but not overwhelming" and how EWF, "a Black group," shouted "Do you feel it" before doing a Sly and the Family Stone routine.[32] One would have to scour YouTube and Facebook videos to see EWF perform "C'mon Children" (from *EWF*), "Time Is on Your Side" (from *LDAT*), "Evil," "Keep Your Head to the Sky" (from *HTTS*), and other crowd-pleasing moments. EWF had already bested Sly's band in New York City so there was no reason for a Sly "routine." Sadly, the tendency of many White music critics to write indifferently and/or inaccurately about EWF and other Black artists exemplifies an unwillingness to honestly engage with Black culture or music. *Esquire* magazine provides a more recent example.

Scott Christian conducted his own 2015 survey of "music festivals" to illustrate the half-century evolution of men's fashion. His example from Cal Jam is a black and white photo of Maurice White in a sequined sleeveless jumpsuit playing the kalimba with a caption on how the excesses of disco and rock reduced music and fashion to one simple matter—flash."[33] White joined many Black musicians from Little Richard to Prince to don exuberant attires to match their vibrant performances. I would contextualize some of the flamboyant outfits worn by EWF members in the historical milieu of Black performative culture. Christian's greater error is his reference to EWF as a progressive rock band. To deploy the label is both intellectually indolent and reductive in drawing attention away from EWF's music to a generic category, which is one of the ideas White's concept for EWF tried to disrupt. I am less concerned about the labels and characterizations—inaccurate or otherwise, Christian and O'Connor use in describing EWF than how both articles epitomize the legacy of journalism about Black music.

The *Esquire* and *The New York Times* articles are examples of the racial premises that unfortunately have undergirded music journalism. Two of these suppositions are worth noting here: (1) Black musicianship is less technically proficient and thus unworthy of serious analysis. (2) Exceptional Black talent resulted from intersections with White music and/or White industry executives. To paraphrase one critic: Black music may be wonderful, but it cannot be considered (intellectually) as legitimate, canonized White music, which pretends to function as a meritocracy without racial considerations.[34] Christian's article is not about music per se, but his description of EWF as a progressive rock band implicitly works from the premise that EWF's success emanated from White "progressive rock" music. More important, none of Christian's twenty "music festivals" from Woodstock in 1969 to 2015's Coachella included a jazz or Black music festival such as New Orleans' Jazz Fest, the *Essence* Festival, Brooklyn's Hip-Hop Festival, Afropunk, or the Harlem Cultural Festival. Apparently, none of these non-White music festivals were worthy inclusions in an article about music and men's fashion.

Until Questlove's recent and poignant *Summer of Soul* which transports viewers to 1969's Harlem Cultural Festival— many writers ignored the significance of the Harlem festival. Christian's article begs several journalistic questions about the Black performers at Harlem's summer festival: How would journalists describe a youthful Stevie Wonder playing drums in a brown suit with a gold ruffled shirt? What would be written about Sly Stone's oversized chain-link gold choker, his multiracial band, and their eclectic music? What prose would portray the Fifth Dimension's music performed in orange fringed vests, red scarfs, and checkered bell-bottomed pants? Perhaps something like, "I should have known they were not white people even though they sounded so." Would writers even attempt to distinguish Nina Simone's braided hair from her conical Afrocentric headpiece? Would her oversized earrings be considered excessive and her African print dress flashy? Journalists avoided these questions by snubbing the festival. Thanks to Questlove—the musician, songwriter, author, and film director whose appreciation of EWF's musical legacy was featured in my prologue—there is one music festival that can no longer be expunged from our collective memories of Black cultural representations.

I emphasized California Jam because of its contextual significance and role in EWF's rise. From the videos I have seen of the festival, those attending were captivated by EWF's unique music and performance. One Facebook post on the California Jam Fan Club gushed about EWF: "They were so good, amazing. I remember the friends I was with were all about waiting for Deep Purple and ELP, but I was glued to watching this amazing performance!" Cal Jam was one performative factor in EWF's breakthrough. Although EWF did not perform "Mighty Mighty" at Cal Jam, the song's chorus would have resonated with the Southern California sun-drenched audience.

## Mighty People

"Mighty Mighty" is indicative of the concept of "tonal semantics" that was influenced by West African tone languages and best understood through music as polytonal expressions. The practice of polytonality allows diverse and complex meanings to be conveyed through sound and music. Like African polyrhythms in general, the polytonal expressions of "Mighty Mighty" are emblematic of African American experiences conveyed in polysemic (multiple meanings) texts.

Another hit song from the album is "Devotion," a ballad sung by Phillip Bailey that expresses EWF's spiritual dimensions. The third hit from *OOE*, "Kalimba Story," conveys EWF's desire to introduce new styles of music through the kalimba. The title selection, "Open Our Eyes," is a gospel tune written by Leon Lumpkins and first recorded in 1959 by the Gospel Clefs. White demonstrated true vocal prowess as the lead on "Open Our Eyes" in what had to be his tribute to Mama and their roots in gospel music. EWF's rendition of "Open our Eyes" is their first (and perhaps only) pure gospel recording and pays homage to the band's—and more significantly, all of African American music's ties to gospel music.

As noted earlier, EWF's themes of self-determination and pride were necessary in part because of the demise of the 1960s Civil Rights Movement. The 1970s brought a void in both the radical and more liberal grassroots organizations for social and political change. Organizations such as the Student Nonviolent Coordinating Committee and the Black

Panther Party were rendered impotent by the state and other political forces. FBI Director J. Edgar Hoover's wiretapping of Dr. King was one component of his counter-intelligence program, also known as COINTELPRO, which dismantled many mainstream Black organizations and their leadership. Black Americans were forced to embark on new strategies in their pursuit of equal justice and opportunity. Voting was one strategy that elected large numbers of Blacks to public offices in many of the same cities that were literally under fire in the previous decade. Black mayors joined Blacks in Congress in mobilizing a national Black political agenda perhaps best embodied by Shirley Chisholm's run for president in 1972.

The aforementioned Black arts movement contributed to new definitions of Blackness and reinforced a greater sense of pride among many African Americans. Film, television and music provided additional cultural images and stories—many embodying a new Black aesthetic consumed by both Blacks and Whites. Even Motown, a testament to Black business success, was forced to refute criticisms of its mass-market sensibilities from a number of fronts, including the mainstream civil rights leadership. The self-proclaimed "sound of young America" was criticized for failing to effectively address Black life in totality.[35] In this context, EWF exemplified a new Black aesthetic fused with a blending of musical traditions that was unprecedented in Black popular music in the 1970s. My contention that EWF's music matters—parallels that of Cornel West's "Black music matters."[36] It matters because Black music has always functioned as a tool to send coded messages to Black people. Dating back to slavery, African oral culture survived in

America and was reinforced through speech patterns and musical expressions of the African people.

Africans managed to maintain their musicality as a significant cultural expression still visible in all forms of Black popular music. Black popular music voices the struggles, faith, and joys of Black people. In this context, Black musicians serve as the village griots, the revisionist historians, and the voices of protest. African American music solidifies the message of the societal concerns of a period by offering snapshots of social conditions and historically defining moments within a society. I also use West's conceptualization of soul music as a starting point in thinking about EWF music. Soul and R&B music constitute more than secularized gospel or funkified jazz. It is the very "Africanization of Afro-American music with intent to appeal to Black masses."[37] One of my earliest first-hand personal encounters with EWF and the power of Black music occurred during my first year in college.

I saw EWF for the second time in May 1974 at my college in Pennsylvania's Pocono mountains. One of the jokes—or rumors—circulating on campus during the heightened anticipation on campus was that the mountainous background on *OOE*'s cover photo was the nearby Poconos. Nobody in the sold-out arena was disappointed in EWF's power-packed show. In fact, I felt a vibe that had yet to exist in the arena or the entire campus community. I noticed even greater on-stage energy from EWF compared to their Uptown Theater performance two years prior. EWF was more polished with greater onstage coordination among the band members. The audience sung-along to "Keep Your

Head to the Sky" and "Devotion," held matches and lighters as we danced to "Power," and the horns of "Mighty Mighty" may have literally brought the house down. I learned years later that in the aftermath of the event, university officials banned future concerts in the arena. At the time nobody was aware of the ban and all we did was talk about the show and sing and dance to EWF music. Many of my friends were surprised by the large numbers of White people in the crowd. Perhaps they failed to consider the concert took place at a predominantly White college. Their surprise certainly underestimated EWF's appeal to non-Black audiences. I witnessed EWF uplift the entire audience in ways no other performers could do. Before *TTWOTW*, the only missing piece in EWF's repertoire was a crossover hit. From Columbia Records' perspective, crossing over was both necessary and inevitable to EWF's national and international success.

## Crossing Over

"Crossover" is a (music/record industry) constructed term applied to musical works or performers who appeal to different types of audiences. In the music industry, a song "crosses over" when it charts on different radio (formats) playlists. I use the term here to connote a song by a Black artist or band that according to the music industry standards of the 1970s, had to be endorsed by Black audiences through Black radio airplay before crossing over to radio stations with predominantly White audiences. Simply put, a top-40 radio station would not play a "Black" record until Black radio stations played them first because of the credence if Black people rejected a song, so too would White people.

In 1995, NBC *Today Show* host Bryant Gumbel credited EWF with inventing crossover. Gumbel's evidence was the success of *TTWOTW*'s "Shining Star" two decades earlier. However, with such crossover hits as Aretha Franklin's "Respect" (1967), Marvin Gaye's "What's Going On" (1971), and a plethora of Motown hits by the Jackson Five and Stevie Wonder, Gumbel's statement lacks merit. Prior to the 1970s, Ray Charles, Sam Cooke, and Chuck Barry were crossing the musical barriers into White audiences. By 1971, Black music recordings were crossing over fairly regularly to the pop charts. Music critic Nelson George argues the 1970s crossover trend led to the "death" of Rhythm & Blues music. Black radio listeners functioned as gatekeepers who auditioned records targeted to White audiences.[38] George acknowledges the various forms of crossover dominated all discussions of Black music, and in his view, the music itself.

Maurice White agrees with this auditioning role but denies creating music for White listeners. Verdine White claims the band never sought to make hits or even get radio play— perhaps a naïve assessment—but his view that as long as EWF was pleased with their music, others would too is echoed by older brother Maurice: "if White audiences were digging us, it was because of the music and our performances. To me it meant we were transcending boundaries."[39] Therefore, EWF's crossover status is both indicative of the music industry's push for crossover Black music in the 1970s and a testament to the band's musicianship.

"Shining Star" was the spark on *TTWOTW* that ignited EWF's breakthrough into the broader and lucrative popular music sphere. Funk was an important ingredient in EWF's musicianship as it was to the success of "Shining Star"—their first crossover hit.

# 5
# Breakthroughs

## Return to Caribou

When EWF returned to Caribou Ranch in late 1974 there were heightened expectations for *TTWOTW*. Pressure came from manager Bob Cavallo who made it clear to White that total fulfillment of his vision was dependent on a mega-successful album. Verdine White also was cognizant of what was at stake for EWF's sixth album because Cavallo had expressed to him and Phillip Bailey the imperative to take it to the next level. More importantly, Maurice White understood his concept of a Black band with universal appeal that promoted personal reflection and pride meant very little Columbia's management. Columbia executives' only concern was that EWF produce a commercially successful album as measured in album sales and radio airplay.

While so many characterize *TTWOTW* as a "breakthrough"—the overused, yet accurate cliché, Bailey uses the term to assess the moment for EWF: "We now had the perfect rhythmic blend for the new music we were about to record." In hindsight, he was right in expecting the album to replace the jazzier elements with an edgier groove, more funk, alongside the new horn and full string sections.[1] EWF reached the Rocky Mountains as a stable and confident band. Maurice White thought the band was solid but knew that everybody had to play with more discipline and focus. His primary mission was to create an environment that generated the creative best from his team. Bailey observed one simple but noticeable change in White's leadership: White assembled the band to explain everyone's parts. This change convinced Bailey *TTWOTW* would be a milestone for EWF.[2]

White realized his vision for EWF would not result from any particular moment or event. Fulfillment of his concept resisted a single performance, song, or even album. I have tried to show how White's concept materialized in stages that encompassed every part of EWF's presentation, from the behaviors of the band members, their live performances, recordings, themes, messages, and album designs. It was impossible for *TTWOTW* to signify a realization of his vision because Maurice's concept continued to evolve after *TTWOTW*. Because Maurice's vision for EWF did not matter to Columbia's execs, EWF's primary goal for *TTWOTW* was to connect with listeners through their collaborative musicianship. The more experienced White and Stepney would lead the process by cultivating each musician's diverse skills into collective outcomes. The creative team believed collaborative production and compositional processes would lead to commercial success.

Despite the band's relative youth and professional inexperience, they were accomplished musicians. For example, Verdine White attended a music conservatory and received formal training as a stand-up bassist. Verdine's most important teacher and mentor was Louis Satterfield, who proclaims Verdine to be a "rhythm king."[3] Phillip Bailey, known by most as a vocalist, is a percussionist who also plays bass and piano. Larry Dunn, like Bailey, was an excellent musician who grew up in a musical family and took classical piano lessons in third grade. As a child, he learned to play guitar, baritone horn, and organ on his way to becoming a virtuoso keyboardist and one of the first musicians to bring the Minimoog to popular music. On *TTWOTW*, Charles Stepney helped Dunn with synthesizer programming and the pair worked together to incorporate the Minimoog on songs and interludes. Despite Stepney's stern treatment and occasional cantankerousness, Dunn respected the composer/arranger as a mentor. Stepney was tough on everyone—especially Dunn, who persevered and respectfully accepted the constructive criticism.[4]

Saxophonist Andrew Woolfolk also coped with Stepney's aggressive coaching as well as White's decision to expand EWF's horn section. As did most of EWF's cohort of skilled musicians, Woolfolk explored a variety of instruments as a teenager which contributed to his versatility as a member of EWF. Woolfolk studied soprano and tenor saxophone, percussion, flute, and honed his vocal talents in a youth gospel choir. Drummer Ralph Johnson's musical upbringing was led by his father, a lyricist, and vocalist mother. There was always music playing in the Johnson home, and Ralph received his first snare drum and drum lessons at the age of eight. His love of R&B music expanded when his brother introduced him to jazz as a teenager. Johnson had to contend with not only Stepney's harsh treatment of young musicians but also the addition of Maurice White's brother Fred as second drummer and White himself who also was a drummer. Johnson dealt effectively with the other drummers because one of his early attractions to drumming came when he attended his first live concert in which James Brown performed with three drum sets on stage.[5]

To enhance the album's production, White brought young recording engineer George Massenburg to Caribou Ranch. White met Massenburg through his friend and guitarist Lowell George—who founded Little Feat—whom like EWF, created music that transcended boundaries with a fusion of rock, folk, blues, rockabilly, country, and soul.[6] Massenburg's skilled recording and engineering techniques helped create EWF's innovative studio sound.

Most reviewers praised the production qualities of *TTWOTW*. *Billboard* characterized the album as a "very tightly produced and performed package" and William Ruhlmann in *The All-Music Guide to Rock* described it as "sleekly produced."[7] Only Gordan Fletcher of *Rolling Stone* criticized the album's "lousy production." Fletcher found the entire album "hot"—which in his view was good for the up-tempo songs and bad for the ballads because they were stifled.[8] Another counterargument to Fletcher's subjective claim is found in George Massenburg's website listing more than ten EWF albums among his nearly 500 album credits as a producer or engineer. Massenburg is recognized for raising the standards of recorded music with his innovations (some heard on *TTWOTW*) and was inducted into the Technology Hall of Fame in 2005.[9]

Hardly objective, Verdine calls the production "stellar" and rates Massenburg as one of the great audio engineers of all time, in the same class as the late Bruce Swedien.[10] Larry Dunn considers Massenburg an absolute genius in terms of using frequencies and sounds that did not clash to the mundane as which microphone is best for a bass drum. Massenburg brilliantly recorded and mixed the numerous layers of Stepney's arrangements and Maurice White's compositions. EWF's success in working with a White recordist who rose to the cutting edge of recording in the 1970s is indicative of Maurice White's collaborative concept for EWF to transcend racial and other demographic constructions.

In terms of *TTWOTW*'s composition, White was the main producer and involved directly in every stage of the process. Stepney served as co-producer and arranger and was usually by White's side throughout. Although every song on *TTWOTW* was composed differently, the music always preceded the lyrics. The band followed a process of developing skeletons of songs and taking those ideas into the studio to allow for improvisation. There may be some truth to the criticisms of the band's songwriting, but quality musicianship and production overcame sporadic writing flaws. Each song could be recorded as many as 8–10 times and Maurice usually picked the best take during mixing. This gave Stepney a solid foundation to add orchestrations which would be followed by keyboard and synthesizer overdubs. For example, Dunn would double Verdine's bass note for note with his Moog bass to give it a more robust sound. Maurice and Philip would spend several days adding their vocals followed by Maurice, Stepney, and Massenburg in the studio doing the final mix.

Maurice co-wrote all but one of *TTWOTW*'s eight songs, and Phillip Bailey co-wrote five. The two were virtually inseparable co-writers but did not follow a prescribed process. According to Bailey, they would often switch responsibility for composing music and lyrics. In fact, Bailey's theory of creativity has three levels—intuitive, development, and fruition. He combines this theory with Stepney's three-stage approach to originality—imitation, assimilation, and creativity.[11] Bailey, White, and the rest of EWF realized that neither the process nor approach will make a difference if you don't have a message or something to communicate. This simple fact applies to both the lyrics and music. Guitarist Al McKay gives an example of his co-writing method with White in simpler terms. McKay would be in the tuning room prior to an EWF performance and White would hear him playing, start to sing something, and ask what he was playing: "I'd say, 'Nothing', He'd say, 'Tape that!' We'd . . . write three or four songs that way. *Big* songs!"[12]

*TTWOTW* was a difficult album for EWF to record. Intermittent with the extended time at Caribou, there were concerts and recording sessions in Los Angeles, mostly for horn overdubs and string recordings. Following his decision to be more accessible, White held conversations with individual members of the band that ranged from professional to personal and spiritual matters. Caribou was ideal for creating because there were few distractions and numerous amenities that included a mess hall available 24/7. With the exception of meals, EWF worked straight through each day for three to four weeks. The band ate breakfast together, moved to the studio around 11 or 12 noon, and recorded until evening dinner. They returned to the studio after dinner to record—sometimes deep into the night. EWF's routine for *TTWOTW* was more intense compared to the relaxed schedule for *OOE* in which the band would record in the afternoons and watch movies at night.

Verdine White noticed how the band's bond with one another grew throughout the process of recording *TTWOTW*. Ralph Johnson attributes the band's chemistry to its success. The diverse musicians that White assembled might not have worked on paper or in theory, but Johnson believes the right musicians were brought together at the right time by the right leader with the right concept.[13] Larry Dunn describes the time as "magical" while Phillip Bailey recalls it as the happiest time for EWF.[14]

### Funk Is Our Own Reward

The mastermind of P-Funk, George Clinton was born one year prior to Maurice White. While both dabbled in doo-wop music at early ages, their musical careers progressed very differently. Clinton—the self-designated authority of funk philosophy, claims finding the funk is synonymous with finding oneself. In "Prelude" from *The Clones of Dr. Funkenstein* (1976), Clinton proclaims "funk is its own reward." Thus, a suitable analytical path for EWF's most successful song on *TTWOTW* is the contention that funk was a factor in EWF's own self-discovery and arc from obscurity to prominence. If funk helped EWF find itself, the band simultaneously brought a level of maturity to funk that made it palatable for the masses.

Maurice, Verdine, and Bailey identify a game-changing incident in 1973 when EWF opened for Clinton's Parliament-Funkadelic in Washington, D.C. Although EWF was accustomed to outperforming other acts on the bill, this time was different. According to Bailey, they "funked us right out of the building!" and in Maurice's words, "Every time we opened the stage door, that funk groove slapped us right in the face . . ." Verdine was more eloquent in telling me, "we got our butts smacked." The humbling experience led to Maurice's challenge to EWF: in order to move audiences—literally and figuratively, a "raw, animalistic, and tribal backbeat" was necessary.[15] In simple musical terms, White deplored EWF to add more funk to its groove.

Despite EWF's humiliation from the funkateers and the rise of funk bands like the Ohio Players, White refused to transform EWF into a funk band, opting once again to remain true to his concept (with minor revisions). He decided to bring back guitarist Al McKay which gave EWF an even stronger rhythm and helped inject elements of funk and "swang" into EWF's up-tempo grooves. McKay—the consummate funk rhythm player—also brought more onstage choreography that enriched EWF's live performances.

In the realm of Black music, the emergence of funk music in the late 1960s replaced R&B and soul music in representing the changing values of African Americans. After the exultation of the civil rights movement faded in the 1970s, funk music represented the social protest discourse of poor and working-class Black youth. The undisputed originator of funk was James Brown—who emphasized the first note or beat in a measure. However, the roots of funk go much deeper. According to Ethnomusicologist Portia Maultsby, the term "funk" comes from the Central African word "lu-funki" and refers to body odor.[16] Funk scholar Rickey Vincent traces funky music to jazz musicians in New Orleans with strong ties to Africa. The very African quality of performing with

> multiple rhythms [laying simultaneously—
> in a lively syncopation—was retained
> [by the slaves at Congo Square]
> and has spread through New Orleans Dixieland Jazz,
> ragtime, rhythm and blues, and ultimately, The Funk.[17]

Other distinguishing characteristics of funk music are integrated polyrhythms—including electric rhythm guitars and pronounced bass rhythms—synthesizers, and independent horn sections. Bootsy Collins (bass) was instrumental in bringing funk's concept of "the One" from Brown's band to Clinton's in 1972. Three years later, Maceo Parker (saxophone) and Fred Wesley (trombone) would follow Collins from Brown to Clinton. Instead of incorporating horns primarily for punctuation as many of the early funk bands (e.g., James Brown, the Bar-Kays) did, Maurice White and Charles Stepney wove them into the foreground of EWF arrangements. In so doing, EWF assisted the rise of horn-based funk bands such as Slave and Brass Construction in the late 1970s and early 1980s.

Although EWF songs like "Mighty Mighty" and "Yearnin' Learnin'" contained these and other characteristics of funk,

I do not characterize EWF as a funk band (as many writers and music critics do).[18] Even Maurice White has been quoted on more than one occasion that EWF never thought of themselves as a funk band: "We always felt we made universal music."[19] Verdine confirmed EWF's incorporation of funk rudiments in their music. Funk is one of the many musical styles woven together in EWF's message-driven music. In the words of music writer Nelson George, EWF "made funk as sweet as funk could be."[20]

Phillip Bailey's memoir differentiates EWF from funk bands like Parliament-Funkadelic and the Ohio Players. He characterizes EWF as a "commercial fusion group" that, unlike funk bands, ran through the cycles of fourths or used bebop horn licks on top of Afro-Cuban rhythms. Larry Dunn's keyboards deployed "big spreads" and extended jazz chords absent from funk bands.[21] EWF's appropriation of funk helped Black music become the dominant form of Black musical expression in the 1970s. EWF's music defies generic labels and classifying it as "R&B" or "funk" obfuscates the essence of their music and the organic connections with diverse audiences they sought to achieve through their music. Similar to "Yearnin' Learnin'," EWF's incorporation of funk was vital to the success of "Shining Star."

### Shining Star

"Shining Star" is the lead track on *TTWOTW* and posits a simple aspirational message that everyone is special in their own way. As the first single released in January 1975, it became

EWF's first number one crossover hit and set the tone for the album's massive success. "Shining Star" earned a Grammy Award for "Best R&B Performance by a Duo or Group with Vocals" (1976). Written by Maurice White, Philip Bailey, and Larry Dunn the 2:50 composition is a danceable, tight, and funk-laced affirmation of human potential that is perfect for commercial radio. The enormous success of "Shining Star," and its importance to *TTWOTW*, compels more detailed analysis than other tracks. I draw from the additional public commentary on this song, perhaps more than any other EWF recording with the possible exception of "September."

Maurice reportedly came up with "Shining Star" during a conversational walk with Bailey one night early in the band's three-week stay at Caribou Ranch. Inspired by the beauty of the stars, White recollects the melody and lyrics that flowed from the pair. For all three writers, composing "Shining Star" was easy because at this stage of the band's collaborative process they knew who EWF was. Their strong bond with their audiences convinced them if they saw themselves as stars, so too could their listeners. The ideas of White and Bailey allowed Larry Dunn to develop the chords and hook on his Fender Rhodes during the unforgettable chorus:

*You're a shining star*
*No matter who you are*
*Shining bright to see*
*What you could truly be*

"Shining Star" opens with two bars of guitarist Al McKay's muffled strings adaptation of an old boogie-woogie ragtime lick in the key of E. He uses a digital delay to get what he describes as a "ticky" effect that pushes the swing to funk (swang). The opening measure is repeated, the second time doubling Verdine's bass guitar. The intro grabs the listener with a syncopated drumbeat/cymbal crash ushers a one-note brass blast. The 0:20 intro ends with improvised vocals, "yeah . . ., hey, hey" followed by a James Brown-style "yep" into the first two lines of the six-line verse which are punctuated by brass stabs: "When you wish upon a star. Your dreams will take you very far, yeah." The last line of the verse is accentuated by falsetto vocal stacking of White and Phillip Bailey: "Life ain't always what it seems, oh yeah." Bailey follows with his vocal bridge to the chorus: "What you see on nights so clear, hey. In the sky so very dear, yeah?"

The groove has a pocket deep enough to bury a 747! McKay believes his feel and groove are his forte: "My gift is finding the pocket. . . . Once I set the pocket, everybody plays to me. I came up with these grooves."[22] One commentator points to the contrast between the verses and the chorus. The verses are firmly rooted in the key of E and contain one measure of vocals followed by one measure of instrumental.[23] Verdine's funky bass riff with tricky fret slides is punctuated by precise drumbeats alongside McKay's rhythm rock guitar. Larry Dunn's short Fender Rhodes licks between choruses are as precious as Johnny Graham's bluesy solo over the horns during the chorus which moves around the circle of fifths. The chorus stands out even more with increased tempo and making each measure two beats of vocals followed by a two-beat pause. Dunn's Fender Rhodes ascends and descends over an E blues scale. McKay's guitar merges with a series of ascending brass chords. The instrumental bridge comes to a hard stop after four bars and a double brass stab followed by the second verse:

*Shining star come into view*
*To shine its watchful light on you . . .*

The sparkling duet reiterates the song's clear-cut message. Dunn and both guitarists insert fusion licks into every space of the second verse. The third verse invokes the reference to sun people from "Mighty Mighty": "Born a man-child of the sun, yeah. Yeah, saw my work had just begun." White hands over to Bailey for a positive reminder:

*So if you find yourself in need . . .*
*Words of wisdom, yes I can.*

The chorus is repeated three times before most instruments drop out (2:38) for White and Bailey's bold acapella ending with handclasps and a few bass licks: "Shining star for you to see. What your life can truly be." On the second phrase, the claps and bass fade out. For the third and final refrain, the vocals are amped and stripped of any echo/compression. The coda sounds like White and Bailey are jumping closer and closer to our ears: "Shining star for you to see. What your life can truly be."

According to sound engineer George Massenburg who oversaw the track's interesting texture, the stark acapella cold ending was Maurice's idea. In Maurice's words, "I wanted the sound to change on the vamp[24], so I told Massenburg to take all the echo off—all the reverb off the vocals—to see what would happen and we liked the sound."[25] For Massenburg, the ending was originally a *slow* fade where the instruments and the reverb gradually disappeared and the four main vocal tracks move right up until they are right in your face . . . so that the song ended in three sections, which were like film "jump cuts".[26]

This ending has the effect of driving the final message with force directly to each individual listener or direct to the listener's ears.

Massenburg initially heard the entire recording as a mess. There was an abundance of tracks to handle, including the recordings in Colorado and those done by Charles Stepney and others in Los Angeles. In addition to cleaning up the vocals and drums, Massenburg fixed Dunn's busy keyboard track. His successful partnership with White and Charles Stepney in mixing "Shining Star" and all *TTWOTW* songs led to a collaboration with EWF that lasted several years. Stepney would co-produce *Gratitude,* EWF's follow-up to *TTWOTW* before passing away during the recording of EWF's next album, *Spirit.*

*Gratitude* was a response to understandable pressure from Columbia for an immediate new release. Fortunately, in developing material for the failed film, EWF recorded many of their concerts. The result was a double album of live and new studio recordings. Released in December 1975, it is inevitable that *Gratitude* contains a live version of "Shining Star" that ends with an extended call-and-response between EWF—"Shining Star"—and the audience, "For you to see":

EWF: *What ya' life*
AUD: *Can truly be*
EWF: *Shining Star*

AUD: *For you to see*
EWF: *What ya' liiiiiiiiiife!*
*Horn Blast!*

Of course, EWF is not the only band or performer to use call-and-response in live shows and recordings. From slave songs to gospel, from bebop to hip-hop, all have made use of call-and-response or antiphony, whether within form, improvisation, instrumental, or vocals. The church is the most common site for call-and-response and most EWF members came from a Black church tradition that made them familiar with antiphony.

In the true spirit of crossing over, "Shining Star" has been sampled by Biggie Smalls, Snoop Dogg, Public Enemy, De La Soul, and the Roots. It has been covered by the Christian glam metal band Stryper, Ruben Stoddard, and numerous marching bands. The recording also was featured in an episode of *Seinfeld* where Elaine (Julia Louis-Dreyfus) embarrasses herself dancing to the hit song. The Bar-Kays, a Memphis-based funk band, imitated "Shining Star" on the introduction of their 1976 single "Too Hot to Stop." Perhaps the greatest testament to the song's impact comes from Stevie Wonder, who has admitted that he imitated the "Shining Star" guitar open (and horns) for his own hit recording, "I Wish."[27]

# 6
# Interludes

No discussion of *TTWOTW* or EWF is complete without attention to the band's interludes—those short musical segments that glide listeners from one song to the next or bring an album (or side) to a close. Once albums replaced 45s (which replaced 78s) in popularity and sales in the mid-1960s, the sequencing of songs on both sides of albums—or in today's parlance, track listing—took on greater importance to most artists and their labels. Effective song sequencing—the flow of one song into another, connecting lyrical content, and the blending of instrumentation—were primary techniques used to keep the listener attentive to each song on an album. EWF's musical segues became a popular staple of their albums and in some cases, live performances.

Most EWF musical interludes are instrumental, although some contain lyrics, chanting, or faint laughter. Larry Dunn and Charles Stepney composed and arranged many of the interludes that showcased Dunn's keyboard/synthesizer wizardry. These interludes enhance the listening experience and heighten anticipation for each track. EWF's interludes also make the actual sequencing of songs less consequential because they contribute to the album's overall aural configuration.

EWF's self-titled debut album followed an R&B practice by such artists as Bobby Womack and Barry White of infusing short monologues or skits between songs. However, these dialogic interludes failed to provide effective humor or meaningful transitions and were discontinued in the follow-up, *TNOL*. Ayanna Dozier's superb analysis of Janet Jackson's *The Velvet Rope* acknowledges the tradition of interludes in Black cultural production as a means to insert drama, role play, and criticism into cultural space. Jackson's use of interludes as an auditory reprieve for listeners provides additional insights into the album's flow and meaning.[1] Interludes have become more common and diverse in contemporary hip-hop with skits, short sermons, swatches of music or sound, and even sprawling instrumentals.

In 2018 *Billboard*'s staff declared the era a "golden age" for the interlude: "the half songs that provide the connective tissue for the marquee pop albums of our time." Since artists such as The Weeknd, Rihanna, and Kendrick Lamar have made interludes fixtures in their work, the magazine ranked its fifty top interludes of all time. Interludes could not exceed a length of 2:50 while skits and spoken-word interludes were not counted. Album openers and closers were also eliminated from contention. In short, interludes are like short songs that make us want more. Rihanna's 2011 "Birthday Cake" topped the list with EWF's 1977 "Brazilian Rhyme (Beijo)" in second place (discussed later). Led Zeppelin's "Bron-Yr-Aur" (1975), Beyoncé's "Yoncé" (2013), and Public Enemy's "Show 'Em What you Got" (1988) rounded out the top five.[2]

EWF's musical interludes began after the band's makeover and Columbia debut. *LDAT* included three Interludes, simply named "Interlude" 1, 2, and 3: the first, "Interlude, No. 1," is a 0:24 Ronnie Laws free-jazz saxophone solo; "Interlude, No. 2" is a 0:24 Larry Dunn classic ragtime piano riff parodying Bent Fabric's "Alley Cat"; and "Interlude, No. 3" is a 53-second lush symphonic orchestration that begins and ends with fades of children's voices playing outdoors. Unlike the first two interludes, "No. 3" provides a melodic segue into Verdine White's bass riff at the start of "Where Have All the Flowers Gone." The others are enjoyable but function mostly as a musical fill between songs. *HTTS* does not have any interludes, but the album ends with a reprise of the final high-pitched measure of "Keep Your Head to the Sky." *OOE* has a 31-second interlude titled "Rabbit Seed," comprised of African chants and drums.

All interludes in *TTWOTW* are unnamed, serving as a prelude or coda to a particular song. For instance, the up-tempo "Happy Feelin'" is followed by an 18-second Larry Dunn Minimoog slow- tempo solo that segues his piano intro in "All About Love." That same melody follows "All About Love" in a longer (1:05) interlude with a soothing, cosmic vibe in the vein of Chick Corea with a cold ending. The album finishes on a similar note (literally) with an interlude after "See the Light." This 40-second interlude has Dunn's same melody as the previous interlude (a slightly faster tempo) but is accentuated by a chanting African ensemble with Dunn's Minimoog mixed underneath as a music bed.

In lieu of the previous interlude's cold end, laughter from the African ensemble closes out the album. This closing interlude's combination of historicized and then-modern technology provides a captivating reinforcement of EWF's goal to connect listeners to Africa, in this case, sub-Saharan Africa. Robert Christgau describes it in his (B+) review of *TTWOTW*: "the taped-in-Africa Matape Ensemble, whose spontaneous laughter closes out the coda, versus Maurice White, whose humorless platitudes prove there is more to roots than tuning a mibra into an ersatz vibraphone."[3] I've already discussed my regard for most music writers, suffice to credit Christgau for at least offering an opinion, unlike most reviewers who ignored them.

EWF assigned titles to most of their interludes after *TTWOTW*: the studio recordings on *Gratitude* have two interludes: "Interlude #1"—a 15-second chant by EWF vocalists—and "Interlude #2"—a 27-second up-tempo guitar-drum riff that precedes "Can't Hide Love." *Spirit* included a :27 interlude titled "Departure," *All N' All* (*ANA*) contained "In the Marketplace (Interlude)" and arguably the most popular EWF interlude, the aforementioned "Brazilian Rhyme (Interlude)," also known as "Beijo." "Brazilian Rhyme" begins with a slow fade of finger-snaps paired with a few Larry Dunn synthesizer chords. Maurice White's and Phillip Bailey's falsettos drive a catchy melody:

*Ba da Ba Ba Ba Ba Ba*
*Ba da Ba Ba Ba*
*Ba da Ba Ba Baw*
*Ba Di Ah Ba Di Aah*

*Ba di Aah EeeAahEeeAah*
(Entire verse repeated)

At :30, drums, bass guitar, and background horns push the groove as Bailey's and White's syncopated stacked vocals harmonize:

*BoBa Da*
*BoBa Da*
*BoBa DaDa*
*BoBa Da Da*
*BoBa Da Da*
(Entire verse repeated)

The 1:20 interlude slow fades to a close with licks from Johnny Graham's bluesy guitar and Verdine White's bass.

"Brazilian Rhyme"—"Beijo," which is Portuguese for "kiss"—has enjoyed a long shelf life. EWF performed it live in 1980 in Rio De Janeiro and included it as a bonus track on the 1999 Legacy reissue. "Brazilian Rhyme (Beijo)" was covered by bass guitarist Marcus Miller and by Take 6 ("Badiyah (Interlude)"). EWF's version has been sampled by a variety of rap and hip-hop artists such as MC Shy D, A Tribe Called Quest, and Blackstreet. In addition to *Billboard*'s recognition, a group of *Rolling Stone* writers in 2016 listed the 80-second interlude among EWF's twelve essential songs.[4]

There are two interludes titled "Brazilian Rhyme" on *ANA*. "Beijo" (Track 6) is followed by a 0:53 "Brazilian Rhyme" (Track 10) that bears no resemblance to the first. *ANA* credits Brazilian singer-songwriter Milton Nascimento with writing both versions. Nascimento is a multi-instrumentalist, known globally as one of the most influential and talented Brazilian musicians. White was inspired by Nascimento when he met him on a 1977 trip to South America that included a stop in Brazil. "Brazilian Rhyme" (Track 10) is a 0:53 slow-tempo airy orchestral composition that was first released by vocalist Elis Regina in 1974 under the title "Ponta De Areia." "Ponta De Areia-Brazilian Rhyme (Interlude)" was a 2:00 interlude on EWF's 1992 compilation *Eternal Dance*. Brazilian musician Eumir Deodato—who also met Maurice White during his 1977 visit to Rio De Janeiro—served as conductor/arranger for the 2:00 recording.

The lyrics of "Brazilian Rhyme"—"Beijo" represent a fundamental principle of Maurice White's songwriting to never let lyrics get in the way of a groove. The late songwriter Allee Willis called this the most important lesson she learned during the writing of EWF's mega-hit, "September."[5] Like the "Ba-Dee-ya, Say do you remember" in "September," there are other verses in EWF songs that may appear nonsensical, yet are pleasing to the ear, and perhaps the entire body. The best example of White's belief that lyrics should enhance the groove and not disrupt it is illustrated by another interlude of sorts involving members of EWF.

## Sun Goddess

Between the 1974 release of *OOE* and *TTWOTW* in 1975, Maurice White called Ramsey Lewis about a couple of recordings that he did not include on *OOE* and believed were better suited for his mentor. White claimed one song would be bigger than "The 'In' Crowd" and naturally Lewis was interested. Maurice, Verdine, Johnny Graham, and Phillip Bailey went to Chicago and joined Ramsey Lewis, Cleveland Eaton, Charles Stepney and others in the studio. The musicians spent three to four days trying to perfect White's much-ballyhooed "Hot Dawgit" into a 3-minute recording.

Finally satisfied with the recording, Maurice remembered his second song, styled as a jazzy instrumental with an R&B, Brazilian feel. White summoned the keyboardist to play the Fender Rhodes solo and former Crane College roommate Don Myrick to play the tenor sax solo.[6] The untitled track emerged from a song White co-wrote with John Lind and was recorded in less than one day. Maurice thought the melody needed some lyrics so he and Phillip Bailey recorded the following vocals that kept the melody in the pocket and flowed with the smooth groove:

*W-a-y oh, w-a-y oh,*
*bop bop way-oh, way-oh-oh*
*Bop-bi-da, ba-ba-ba-bah-di-ay-oh*
*Bop-bop way-oh, way-ah-oh*
*Ah . . . ah-ah . . . Ah-ah . . .*

Before those soothing harmonies, the song begins with Graham's rhythm guitar pacing the 0:50 introduction with Verdine's bass, Stepney's synthesizer, and of course, Lewis' Fender Rhodes. Not that any listener could miss the ensuing percussion, 10 seconds in, Maurice (in the control room) says, "I want to put another rhythm part in it." The engineer asks him where he wants to put the claves (a pair of cylindrical hardwood sticks) and White replies, "On the solo." White's phrase remained on the recording that was named "Sun Goddess" which became the album's title track. Lewis' Fender Rhodes solo elevated the groove to lift "Sun Goddess" to his first hit record nearly ten years after "The 'In' Crowd."

How White came up with the name "Sun Goddess" may forever remain a mystery, so I offer brief speculation. Most people think of Gods and Goddesses as being a Greek thing. However, keeping in mind the importance of light for EWF discussed earlier, the sun goddesses represent the power and force of the light of the sun. There are close to twenty-five different sun goddesses from around the world, including Aboriginal, Sri Lankan, Japanese, Native American, and of course several from Greece and Egypt.

Regardless of White's motivation to name the song "Sun Goddess," it clearly has the elements of an EWF song. The jazz-inflected, uplifting melody, Latin-laced rhythm guitar groove, and catchy harmonized vocals should have indicated to White the song had potential as a hit despite the solos by Lewis and Myrick that extended the recording to 8:30, which under most circumstances would disqualify a song from radio airplay. White overlooked the length because he deemed it as a jazz recording that would not be released as a single.

White underestimated "Sun Goddess" and suggested Lewis release "Hot Dawgit" as a single, only to see it tank. The album became a smash because of "Sun Goddess" despite White's initial refusal to edit the song. Columbia Records eventually released a 45 rpm version of "Sun Goddess" which everyone identified as EWF. The album became a certified crossover hit, reaching No.1 on the *Billboard* Black Albums chart, No. 1 on the jazz chart, and No. 12 on the pop chart.

Although "Sun Goddess" was promoted as a collaboration between Ramsey Lewis and EWF, it belonged more to EWF. The song's success brought a larger budget from Columbia for *TTWOTW*, and perhaps some new fans to Ramsey Lewis and EWF. A 7:41 live version was one factor in the success of EWF's double album *Gratitude* released in December 1975. For several years, the song remained popular on EWF tours, with Larry Dunn more than capably assuming Lewis' keyboards. Lewis joined EWF on tour in 1975 after the release of *TTWOTW*, the band's most celebrated album.

# 7
# International Anthem

I save the title selection for last because it became the anthem Maurice sought since his days with Ramsey Lewis when he began to develop his concept. After Maurice's stepfather, Verdine Sr., bestowed the moniker of "national anthem" to "That's the Way of the World" ("TTWOTW"), Maurice would often introduce it in live performances as EWF's national anthem. White believed the song epitomized EWF's divine mission to share hopeful messages with the world. "TTWOTW" asks people not to give up hope regardless of how hopeless the world could be.[1]

According to Verdine, "TTWOTW" materialized from Maurice's insistence that band members collaborate in song composition. He described the writing process as a fluid method between himself, Maurice, and Charles Stepney, with the two White brothers writing the lyrics and Stepney, Dunn, and Bailey working on the arrangement.[2] One intention of the successful composer, writer, or arranger is to map meanings of human experience sonically.[3] Efficacious music—lyrics, vocals, arrangements, solos, and stage performances—often relays shared cultural values or respond to cultural needs. Such is the case with "TTWOTW."

EWF's anthem was created out of necessity—for the band, its creative team, the country, and the world. As the Vietnam War neared an unsuccessful end, Watergate drained Americans' faith in its government, Maurice was convinced people needed to hear this hopeful song as much as he needed to sing it. Stepney's arrangement of melancholy, yet buoyant, chord changes resonated during a time when many citizens were discouraged by the status quo. Collectively, "TTWOTW"'s lyrics, chord changes/repetitions, guitar solos, and rolling horn lines offer an uplifting message about the benefits (i.e., peace of mind) of staying true to oneself.

White's designation of "TTWOTW" as a "national anthem" invites listener participation in a cultural ritual of shared meaning. Audience engagement is achieved in numerous ways such as recognizable grooves, "singable" melodies, "danceable" rhythms, and familiar refrains. The song establishes a sonic communal experience that is found in every pass of the main melodies, the background sing-along verses, the meditative chords, and the lyrics. Although "TTWOTW" was commissioned as a film score, the composition bears no connection to the motion picture and the songwriters ostensibly paid no attention to the screenplay.

Released as a single three months after the release of the album, "TTWOTW" peaked at number five on *Billboard*'s Hot Soul Singles and twelve on the *Billboard* Hot 100. Critical reviews of the song, like the album, were overwhelmingly positive.[4] "TWTOTW" is a smooth medium tempo recording with a soulful groove style in the Black music tradition. It begins on the beat immediately after the piercing cold ending to "Shining Star." The 5:45 recording opens with Larry Dunn's sprinkling Fender Rhodes and light cymbal taps escorted by Verdine's electric bass guitar. The lightly textured instrumentation sways to meditative horn lines and faint percussion (snare and triangle) in the opening eight bars. The tone is mellow and soothing with a touch of sparkle as the swaying horns gently glide the listener along the (0:36) introduction's airy groove that floats into the first chorus' layered falsetto vocals:

> *Hearts afire, creates love desire*
> *Take you high and higher*
> *To the world you belong . . .*
> *To your place on the throne.*

Lyrically, "TTWOTW" resembles a short, gentle sermon delivered by White and Bailey. White uses his earthy tenor that included a high-to-low octave blend, while Bailey compliments White with his rich falsetto. White developed his own falsetto after Bailey joined the ensemble and the two developed harmonies akin to Sérgio Mendes & Brasil '66 (sans the bossa nova) but distinctive enough to create EWF's signature vocal style. Bailey and White's vocal style in "TTWOTW" is reminiscent of that deployed in "Shining Star" only softer and smoother.

With sermon-like lyrics, the instrumentation gives the song a "churchy" feel of relaxed worshippers at a unified gathering to share a hopeful sermon. Bailey and White sing the first verse: "We've come together on this special day . . . (huh). Sing a message loud and clear (hmm, mm)." Unification is achieved partly via subtle call-and-response vocal reinforcement when the lead earns a retort from background vocals. Unity also is reached through empathetic identification as White and Bailey remind listeners they too have faced troubled times that dissipate. The harmonized vocals during the bridge personify inner peace through introspection: "You will find (you will find), Peace of mind (yeah, haaa), if you look way down, In your heart and soul." The brief call-and-response creates a shared concern and common struggle—an ethos the lead vocalists acquired from their gospel traditions. The harmonized vocal scaling inspires listeners to take matters into their own hearts which provides a sense of redemption in a troubled world: "Ahh, don't hesitate, 'Cause the world seems cold. Stay young at heart, Ahh, 'cause you're never old at heart, never, never, never, never, never, never." The peppered harmonized vocals—"stay young at heart"—deliver the appropriate idiom because it connotes a youthful disposition consonant with listeners of any age. White and Bailey impel the chorus' call-and-response:

> *That's the way (that's the way)*
> *Of the world (of the world)*
> *Plant your flower (gonna plant your flower)*
> *And you grow a pearl (heeey, ooh, ooh, ooh)*

Short ad-libs and vamps begin at 2:25 and furnish a Black gospel sound quality that is solidified with references to the Lord: "Oooooh, ooh, ha, Lord. Can't you see, me y'all?" In pure musical terms, a vamp is an accompaniment to a solo voice or instrument. Commonly deployed in jazz, the term "vamp till ready" signals the accompanist to repeat one or two passages until the soloist is ready. Vamps also are often heard at the end of soul/R&B recordings when vocal effects such as rapid scales and improvised passages are faded out. EWF's vamps lead into a 30 second instrumental bridge highlighted by guitarist Johnny Graham's blues riff of tantalizingly haunting chords. His solo adds an earthy texture for a reflective moment before the chorus' recap.

In the essence of a sermon, the lyrics resist a pure repetition of the first verse with a subtle change in tense that is barely noticeable. The first verse's reference to "coming" together to "sing" is replaced with "We came together . . . sung our message . . . ," denoting their message has been conveyed. The final minute and one half reprise the bridge and chorus with White's repeated ad-libs: "that love, that love, that love . . ." Like most sermons, "TTWOTW" ends with a short prayer: "Lordy won't you hear me now? Lordy, won't you hear me now?" The song fades with ad-libs.

The song calls for personal agency in a troubled world and does not identify any particular social issue. Listeners are summoned to empower themselves in the world through their own humanity. To "plant your flower" is a call to establish or embed, in this context, self-reflection and personal development. The flowers we nurture are our inner beauties, compassions, and capacities to love. The pearls we grow imply our beauty, wisdom, or generosity. Pearls are believed to give people a sense of inner confidence that allows them to take on life's challenges. Our quest for peace of mind and love will lead us to our rightful place in the world. Although thrones are usually reserved for gods, kings, or queens, they are evoked in religious sermons to encourage an understanding of God's word and partnership with the Lord. Inner peace is the reward for taking heed of this message and remaining true to self.

During a 1981 ABC television interview, Maurice White offered his take on one line from *TTWOTW*'s chorus that stood out to him: "Children are born with a heart of gold; way of the world makes his heart grow cold." Without conceding the apparent bitterness from living in a troubled world that is implied in the passage, he adds with a chuckle, "We've always tried to help—make that a lie." White implies that EWF's mission to impact the world in positive ways would help ameliorate a world that may appear to render little hope. EWF's aspirational message of remaining true to oneself (as the band was doing) challenges the harsh ways of the world. "TTWOTW" creates shared spaces for positive (love) desires.

The song's captivating instrumentation reinforces its straightforward message of hope. The references to hearts afire, pearls, and flowers became easy targets for accusations of cosmic drivel or gibberish. As an academic familiar with excessive jargon and circumlocution "TTWOTW"'s lyrics are down-to-earth. Everyone can relate to flowers and pearls and everybody seeks inner peace. Their message of hope is necessary because the innocence and purity associated with children *can* be tainted in adults by social conditions. EWF's implication for listeners to remain true to themselves coincided with the band's approach to the entire album.

Maurice successfully disassociated the album from the film. Instead of creating songs in line with the film's critique of the music industry—which would have been easy given the band's experiences—EWF crafted songs about what they believed listeners needed to hear and would benefit from.[5] White won a dispute with Columbia Records over his refusal to have the standard label, "The Original Motion Picture Soundtrack," printed boldly on the front cover. Although the soundtrack label did appear in small lettering on the back cover, White's intuition proved correct when the band was distraught after attending the film's screening. The film had an awful story line and weak acting—including the limited parts from EWF. As a result, the film received no advanced promotion and only made it to a handful of theaters before dying in a few days. Even though the film was distributed by United Artists, it remained buried until 2006 when it was released on DVD.

Without panic EWF resumed final preparations for the album's release and chose noted South African photographer Norman Seeff to shoot the album cover. Known for his outstanding black and white photographs of such luminaries as Steve Jobs, Tina Turner, Joni Mitchell, and Miles Davis, Seeff lent his mastery to *TTWOTW*'s gatefold. Some band members appear standing or in dance poses, others in mid-air, and all against a white backdrop. There are no photographs from the film that bombed and never reached enough theaters to undermine the album or EWF's career. Compared to other EWF album covers, *TTWOTW*'s black and white photography depicts the band's most basic motif. EWF band members are pictured gleefully perhaps knowing the album was independent from the failed film and the music judged on its own merits.

EWF performed "TTWOTW" live during its 1975 *TTWOTW* tour. In an incontrovertible evocation of the song's sermonized underpinning, White introduces "TTWOTW" as "an old-time church groove" and adds several references to church as the song closes. Reminiscent of a church service, White beckons his congregation to clap while he preaches:

> *Now I'ma take you all the way back*
> *to the front row seat where they used to testify.*
> *There was a time, when they didn't have any instruments,*
> *all they had was this soul, the moving of their bodies.*
> *So I want to feel you clap your hands. Give me the spirit.*

He leads concertgoers in a call-and-response as they respond in near-perfect unison to his verse: "That's the Way" with, "Of the World." This and other performances, such as their September 1975 European tour with Columbia labelmate Santana, solidified "TTWOTW" as EWF's international anthem. The European tour also imparted one musician with a career-altering inspiring introduction to EWF.

Jean-Paul Maunick saw EWF perform in Germany. He claims he went to see Santana, but EWF mesmerized and left him "gobsmacked for the entire show. I don't think I closed my mouth. Maurice White's kalimba—it was . . . mystical. EWF opened my mind to all possibilities. . . . To see these guys made me play what I'd play in my career, with horns, percussion."[6] Maunick, better known as "Bluey," formed the British band Incognito in 1979. Incognito, like EWF, mixes soul, funk, and jazz via Bluey's soulful rhythm guitar, male and female vocalists, and big horns. For EWF and Incognito, the whole is greater than the sum of their many talented parts. There is little doubt that EWF inspired other musicians from around the world.

# Epilogue

*TTWOTW* was successful both commercially and artistically in fusing musical styles and offering uplifting messages to people in a troubled world. If *TTWOTW* altered people's lives, it was not by telling them *how* to live but by promoting personal pride and self-reflection as ways people *can* live. To this day, EWF's band members remain convinced their music touched the hearts, minds, and souls of listeners. They recall fan testimonials such as "because of you, I got off heroin" or "your music helped me discover who I could be."

Maurice White formed EWF out of a dual need: his own quest to realize his total potential and a desire to serve humanity. As the previous testimonials indicate, EWF served society with powerful presentations of positive messages of hope and aspiration. *TTWOTW* did not represent fulfillment of White's concept, but it demonstrated its successful evolution. Following their 1975 European tour, EWF promoted *TTWOTW* in the United States to adoring and demographically expanding audiences. Band members noticed more Whites, Latinos, and mixed couples at their concerts. The landmark album was more than a breakthrough for EWF, it contributed to a defining moment in popular music.

EWF's crossover success, mistakenly decried by some critics, provided pathways for artistic success for other musicians. The band's success also led to increasing numbers of African American music industry executives. EWF was the first Black band to earn similar concert revenues to those of White, mostly British acts. With sold-out concerts, EWF called their own shots—booking their own engagements and using Black promoters. The band hired Broadway choreographer George Faison, Hollywood costume designer Bill Whitten, enlisted the magical talents of Doug Henning and David Copperfield to enrich their concert performances, while individual band members obtained commercial endorsements. Maurice established a production company, Kalimba Productions in 1975 and signed his mentor Ramsey Lewis, singer Deniece Williams (a former member of Stevie Wonder's "Wonderlove" backup group), and the Emotions to his company. EWF followed *TTWOTW* with a string of triumphant albums that included *Gratitude*, *Spirit*, *All 'N All*, and *I Am*.

EWF's *Gratitude* is an aptly titled expression of appreciation to their audiences. The title selection adds a thank-you to the Creator:

> *We just wanna give Gratitude*
> *Got plenty love we wanna give to you*
> *With good music and we're tryin' to say*
> *That the Good Lord's gonna make a way.*

In addition to the powerhouse live recordings "Africano/ Power," "Shining Star," "Reasons," "Yearnin' Learnin'," and

"Sun Goddess," the double-album yielded two studio recorded hits, "Sing a Song" and "Can't Hide Love." Notwithstanding EWF's pair of top-selling albums the self-proclaimed arbiter of funk used his own 1975 recording to invoke professional jealously disguised as humor.

Parliament-Funkadelic founder, George Clinton poked fun at EWF on the title track of Funkadelic's 1975 album, "Let's Take It to the Stage." Clinton's lyrics are clever, but rarely profound in mocking popular musicians and parodies of risqué nursery rhymes. His stream-of-consciousness-style rapping referred to EWF as "Earth, hot air and no fire." Clinton's wit put EWF in good company: he renamed Kool & the Gang, "Fool & the Gang," Rufus and Chaka Khan became "Hey Sloofus! Tell Me Something Good!," and he converted Sly and the Family Stone to "Slick and the Family Brick." The equal opportunity musical pundit even took down the originator of funk, James Brown by calling him "James Clown." Returning the friendly play on words, Verdine White delivered a sidesplitting impersonation of George Clinton to me in recounting a conversation the two had years after the P-Funk mob blew away EWF in Washington, D.C. The down-to-earth bass player rightfully finds compliments in Clinton's verbal jabs at EWF.[1]

Few critics, and even fewer musicians, have landed a solid punch on EWF. Even those who characterize their lyrics as "cosmically silly"[2] or "cosmological gobbledygook"[3] find their music and performances beyond reproach. Of the tens of thousands of songwriters in today's era of music, Maurice White is among the approximately 400 inductees into the Songwriters Hall of Fame. To paraphrase Maurice, don't let little lyrics get in the way of a huge groove.

I end on a note similar to my point in the prologue regarding the apolitical nature of EWF's music. The band bridged a political divide, albeit momentarily, as Barack Obama writes in his presidential memoir about the 2009 Governors Ball:

> Michelle (Obama) had shaken up tradition by arranging to have Earth, Wind & Fire provide the entertainment, their horn-blasting funk generating moves on the dance floor that I'd never thought I'd see out of a bipartisan gathering of middle-aged officials.[4]

If only that was the way of the world.

# Notes

## Preface

1. *Rolling Stone.* (October 2020). "That's the Way of the World." *Superseventies.com.* Accessed August 21, 2021. https://www.superseventies.com/spearthwindfire.html. This is the highest standing for *TTWOTW* during *Rolling Stone*'s periodic album ranking.

2. Neil Shah. (February 4, 2016). "Earth, Wind and Fire Founder Maurice White Dies." *Wall Street Journal.* Accessed June 8, 2021. https://blogs.wsj.com/speakeasy/2016/02/04/maurice-white-earth-wind-and-fire-dies/.

3. Verdine White, personal communication (Zoom), April 20, 2021.

4. The passage is from Dr. King's 1967 speech at Stanford University, "The Other America," in which he tried to explain the cause of rioting to a predominantly white audience. King made the often overlooked point that rioting is not exclusive to Black Americans.

5. Mark Anthony Neal. (1999). *What the Music Said: Black Popular Music and Black Public Culture.* New York: Routledge, p. xi.

6    The call-and-response is a form of interaction between a speaker and an audience in which the speaker's statements ("calls") are punctuated by responses from the listeners. It is rooted in African linguistic and musical traditions that provide a pattern of democratic participation in public gatherings. This form is also used in music under the general category of antiphony.

7    James Brown, "Say It Loud – I'm Black and I'm Proud' (1968)." TeachRock.org. "'Alright' and the History of Black Protest Songs." Accessed April 28, 2020. https://3o9d0y1wloj7e90 sc37nviar-wpengine.netdna-ssl.com/wp-content/uploads/DLP -Alright.pdf.

8    Maurice White. (2016). *My Life with Earth, Wind & Fire*. With Herb Powell, New York: Amistad, pp. 64–5.

## Chapter 1

1    M. White, *My Life*, p. 80.

2    M. White, *My Life*, pp. 81–2.

3    M. White, *My Life*, p. 87.

4    Dunn incorporated a more traditional ragtime piano riff, "Interlude #2" on EWF's *Last Days and Time*.

5    David Nathan. (July 1975). "Earth, Wind & Fire: A Creative Explosion." "Earth, Wind & Fire: Classic 1975 Interview + Personal Postscript." Accessed December 24, 2020. https:// www.soulmusic.com/article/earth-wind-fire-classic-1975/. M. White, *My Life*, pp. 13, 14.

6    Booker T. Jones. (2019). *Time Is Tight: My Life Note by Note*. New York: Little Brown and Company, p. 45.

7   M. White, *My Life*, pp. 27–9. B. T. Jones, *Time*, p. 49.

8   M. White, *My Life*, p. 31.

9   M. White, *My Life*, p. 34.

10  Napoleon Hill. (1928). *The Law of Success: The Master Wealth-Builder's Complete and Original Lesson Plan for Achieving Your Dreams.* New York: Penguin Group, p. 92.

11  M. White, *My Life*, p. 35.

12  Vincent recognized the horn sections of EWF and Parliament as embodying the expansive role of horns in a song's primary melody. Rickey Vincent. (2014). *The Music, the People, and the Rhythm of THE ONE.* New York: Macmillan, pp. 17, 19.

13  Andrew Woolfolk (flute, saxophone) was an established member of EWF before its new horn section of Don Myrick (saxophone), Lou Satterfield (trombone), Michael Harris and Rahmlee Michael Davis (trumpets) expanded from the tour to create EWF's powerful horn section, the Phenix horns.

14  The two bands and their horn sections performed together in 2004 and 2016.

15  B. T. Jones, *Time*, p. 49.

## Chapter 2

1   N. Hill, *The Law*, pp. 337, 355.

2   N. Hill, *The Law*, p. 127.

3   M. White, *My Life*, p. 54.

4   Robert Pruter. (1990). *Chicago Soul*. Chicago: University of Illinois Press, p. 123.

5   *Shining Stars: The Official Story of Earth, Wind & Fire*,
    directed by Kathryn Arnold and Stephanie Bennett. London:
    Eagle Rock Entertainment, 2001.

6   Paul Bowler. (No. 516, March 2021). "The Engine Room:
    Charles Stepney." *Record Collector*. Accessed February 9, 2021.
    https://recordcollectormag.com/articles/the-engine-room-4.

7   I watched in amazement Billy Stewart perform at the Uptown
    Theater in the late 1960s.

8   Pruter, *Chicago*, p. 115.

9   Billy Stewart died at the age of thirty-two in an automobile
    accident in 1970. M. White, *My Life*, pp. 54–5.

10  Julieanne Richardson. (June 29, 2004). "Ramsey Lewis: The
    History Makers." (A2001.040).

11  Nick DeRiso. (November 23, 2011). "Ramsey Lewis, Jazz
    Legend: Something Else! Interview." Accessed July 21, 2021.
    https://somethingelsereviews.com/2011/11/23/something-else
    -interview-jazz-legend-ramsey-lewis/.

12  Paul F. Berliner. (1979). *Soul of Mbira: Music and Traditions
    of the Shona People of Zimbabwe*. Oakland: University of
    California Press. Mark Holdaway. (May 26, 2018). "My Story
    of Hugh Tracey—Kalimba Magic." Accessed July 20, 2021.
    www.kalimbamagic.com.

13  Larry Crowe. (January 18, 2007). "Philip Cohran: The History
    Makers." (A2006.158). The History Makers Digital Archive.
    Session 2, tape 10, story 5. Despite Cohran's claim, there is
    no evidence that White was unsuccessful in an effort to join
    the AHE prior to joining Ramsey Lewis in 1966. In addition,
    Verdine White is not credited on any of AHE recordings,
    although his teacher Louis Satterfield did play bass for the
    ensemble.

14 Clovis E. Semmes. (1994). "The Dialectics of Cultural Survival and the Community Artist: Phil Cohran and the Afro Arts Theatre." *Journal of Black Studies*, Vol. 24, No. 1, 447–61.

15 Ericka Blount Danois. (January 22, 2021). "Cosmic Heights: Earth, Wind & Fire." Original publication, Issue 47. *Waxpoestics.com*. Accessed July 19, 2021. https://www.waxpoestics.com/article/earch-wind-and-fire-cosmic-heights.

16 White incorporated a similar kalimba melody in a musical interlude on EWF's 1983 *Powerlight* album.

17 M. White, *My Life*, p. 191.

18 E. B. Danois, "Cosmic Heights."

19 M. White, *My Life*, p. 74.

20 M. White, *My Life*, p. 66.

21 N. Hill, *The Law*, p. 171.

22 M. White, *My Life*, p. 83.

23 White's memoir inexplicably misspells Riperton's name ("Ripperton") in his brief reference to her in his discussion of Charles Stepney.

24 I look forward to Brittnay L. Proctor's 33 1/3 examination of Riperton's *Come to My Garden*. Perhaps the book will shed light on the unknown lyrics in the second verse of "Les Fleurs."

## Chapter 3

1 N. Hill, *The Law*, p. 9.

2 V. White, personal communication, 2021.

3 V. White, personal communication, 2021.

4   Lester Bangs. (June 24, 1971). "Earth, Wind & Fire." (album review). Accessed June 12, 2020. https://www.rollingstone .com/music/albumreviews/earth-wind-fire-19710624.

5   The self-proclaimed "dean" of American rock critics is known for his disdain for a variety of music including salsa, dance, jazz fusion, and gospel. I find his terse, letter-graded capsule reviews of albums more maddening than provocative. Christgau was ambivalent toward EWF's musical "cross references" with expert "vocal harmonies" that defy the concept. He found the kalimba "weird" and gave the album a C+. Robert Christgau (1971). "Earth, Wind & Fire: Earth, Wind & Fire." (album review). *Village Voice*. Accessed May 13, 2020. https://www.robertchristgau.com.

6   Bruce Lindsey. (July 13, 2019). "Earth, Wind & Fire: Earth, Wind and Fire/The Need of Love." (album review). *Jazz Journal*. Accessed May 13, 2020. https://jazzjournal.co.uk/2019/07/13/ earth-wind-and-fire-earth-wind-and-fire-the-need-of-love/.

7   *Baadasssss!* (2003) (film). Maria Van Peebles, director. Van Peebles appeared in his father's film as a child.

8   E. B. Danois, "Cosmic Heights."

9   *Shining Stars: The Official Story of Earth, Wind & Fire.*

10  E. B. Danois, "Cosmic Heights."

11  M. White, *My Life*, pp. 95–6.

12  "I Think About Lovin You" was the song that introduced me and perhaps millions of radio listeners to EWF.

13  E. B. Danois, "Cosmic Heights."

14  Scott Goldfine. (February 2018). "Truth in Rhythm." Scott Goldfine interviews Larry Dunn interview, Part 1. Accessed April 24, 2021. https://www.youtube.com/watch?v=_e6uVcpuG_U.

15   Phillip Bailey. (2014). *Shining Star: Braving the Elements of Earth, Wind & Fire*. With Keith Zimmerman and Kent Zimmerman. New York: Penguin Group, pp. 83, 85.

16   M. White, *My Life*, p. 84.

17   P. Bailey, Shining Star, p. 153.

18   P. Bailey, *Shining Star*, p. 163.

# Chapter 4

1   White's memoir claims the audience booed, threw objects, and laughed (p. 109). A similar account is detailed in Bailey's book with quotes of hostile heckling and booing that eventually gave way to cheers (pp. 7, 113). Perhaps they were referring to a different show then the Sunday afternoon performance I attended.

2   P. Bailey, *Shining Star*, p. 7.

3   Leonard Smith is credited with starting an EWF ritual of gathering the band in a circle of prayer before a stage performance. He also shielded White and band members from the many outside distractions they encountered over the years.

4   Clive Davis. (2013). *The Soundtrack of My Life*. New York: Simon & Schuster, p. 157.

5   Columbia Records' parent company CBS had secured a unique partnership with Philly sound pioneers Kenneth Gamble and Leon Huff with the 1971 launch of Philadelphia International Records.

6   P. Bailey, *Shining Star*, p. 108.

7   M. White, *My Life*, p. 116.

8    David Ritz. (2002). "Middle C in the Sky." liner notes for *Earth, Wind & Fire that's the Way of the World: Alive in '75.*

9    P. Bailey, *Shining Star*, p. 108.

10   C. Davis, *Soundtrack*, p. 158.

11   P. Bailey, *Shining Star*, pp. 113–14.

12   M. White, *My Life*, p. 119.

13   C. Davis, *Soundtrack*, p. 158.

14   Phillip Bailey confirmed the passing of Andrew Woolfolk, 71, on April 24, 2022. Woolfolk was the EWF saxophonist from 1973 to 1985, and from 1987 to 1993.

15   Gayle Wald. (2015). *It's Been Beautiful: Soul! And Black Power Television.* Durham: Duke University Press, p. 5.

16   Gayle Wald. (February 7, 2009). "The History of SOUL! and Influence of Host Ellis Haizlip." *Inside Thirteen.* Accessed February 4, 2022. https://www.thirteen.org/blog-post/history -soul-show-host-ellis-haizlip/.

17   M. White, *My Life*, p. 134.

18   P. Bailey, *Shining Star*, pp. 121–2.

19   *Shining Stars: The Official Story of Earth, Wind & Fire.*

20   M. White, *My Life*, p. 130.

21   Indiana University, Bloomington. (2012–2013). "Liner Notes: Logan Westbrooks: Music Industry Executive, Entrepreneur, Teacher, Philanthropist." *Archives of African American Music and Culture.* Accessed August 21, 2021. https://aaamc.sitehost .iu.edu/liner-notes-pdfs/linernotes17.pdf.

22 M. A. Neal, *What the*, p. 117. C. Davis, *Soundtrack*, p. 157.

23 Anonymous. (July 31, 2020). "How Did Major Record Companies Take Control of Black Music?" *Cleeze Report*. Accessed August 21, 2021. https://cleezereport.com/f/how -did-major-record-companies-take-control-of-black-music ?blogcategory=Anonymous.

24 M. White, *My Life*, p. 118.

25 Wayne Edwards. (2015). *Can't Touch This: Memoir of a Disillusioned Music Executive*. Bloomington, IN: AuthorHouse.

26 P. Bailey, *Shining Star*, pp. 134–5.

27 The retort sounds more like Larry Dunn than Maurice White. S. Goldfine. "Truth in Rhythm: Larry Dunn interview."

28 M. White, *My Life*, p. 148.

29 M. White, *My Life*, p. 133.

30 CNN, *The Seventies*. "What's Going On." *CNN*. Episode 8, Original broadcast, August 8, 2015. Rebroadcast July 11, 2021.

31 M. White, *My Life*, pp. 113–14.

32 John J. O'Connor. (May 9, 1974). "TV 'California Jam' Simulates Live Rock Session." Accessed June 3, 2020. https:// www.nytimes.com/1974/05/09/archives/tvcalifornia-jam -simulates-live-rock-session-in-concert-presents.html.

33 Scott Christian. (October 19, 2015). "These 20 Music Festival Photos Chronicle a Half-Century of Style." *Esquire*, Accessed June 12, 2020. https://www.esquire.com/style/mens-fashion/ g2463/music-festival-style/.

34 My reading and research for this book came across countless articles guilty of these and other racist premises. Scott Woods'

insightful analysis of music journalism situates EWF music as a litmus test for discussions of racism. (April 7, 2021). "Don't Talk to Me About Racism if You Don't Know Earth, Wind & Fire's Catalog." *Level*, Accessed May 10, 2021. https://level .medium.com/dont-talk-to-me-about-racism-if-you-don-t -know-earth-wind-fire-s-catalog-facdf624cbd9.

35  M. A. Neal, *What the*, pp. 45–7.

36  Cornel West. (2007). "Berklee College of Music Website." Accessed May 12, 2020. https://college.berklee.edu/.

37  Cornel West. (2007). "Lecture at Berklee College of Music's Africana Studies Inauguration." Accessed July 22, 2021. https://college.berklee.edu/focused/africana.

38  Nelson George. (1988). *The Death of Rhythm & Blues*. New York: Penguin.

39  M. White, *My Life*, p. 182. White also notes the importance a hit record to everybody in the music business and his acknowledgment of a hit song's impact on a band's morale contradicts Verdine's position.

## Chapter 5

1  P. Bailey, *Shining Star*, p. 135.

2  P. Bailey, *Shining Star*, pp. 135, 137.

3  *Shining Stars: The Official Story of Earth, Wind & Fire*.

4   The two became so close that Dunn presented Stepney with his gold record for *TTWOTW*. S. Goldstein, "Truth in Rhythm."

5   National Association of Music Merchants (NAMM). (September 2, 2014). "Ralph Johnson Interview." Accessed July 29, 2021. https://www.namm.org/library/oral-history/ralph-johnson.

6   Similar to EWF, Little Feat was formed in Los Angeles, signed with Warner Bros., endured several personnel changes, but remained with Warner Bros until 1980, when the band disbanded after the death of Lowell George.

7   *Rolling Stone*. (October 2020). "That's the Way of the World."

8   Gordon Fletcher's *Rolling Stone* review found the production lacking. (July 3, 1975). "That's the Way of the World." *Rolling Stone.com*. Accessed April 23, 2020. https://www.rollingstone .com/music/music-album-reviews/thats-the-way-of-the -world-205609/amp/.

9   Accessed April 23, 2020. https://www.massenburg.com/.

10  V. White, personal communication, 2021.

11  P. Bailey, *Shining Star*, pp. 136–7.

12  Oscar Jordan. (January 17, 2011). "5 Funk Guitarists You Should Know." *Premier Guitar*. Accessed August 18, 2015. http://www.premierguitar.com/articles/5_Funk_Guitarists _You Should Know.

13  "Ralph Johnson" (September 2, 2014). NAMM Interview with Ralph Johnson. Accessed December 29, 2021. https://www .namm.org/library/oral-history/ralph-johnson.

14  Chris Williams. (February 8, 2012). "Key Tracks: Earth, Wind & Fire's That's the Way of the World. Larry Dunn Talks about the Group's Multi-Platinum Smash." Accessed April 23, 2021. https://daily.redbullmusicacademy.com/2016/02/key-tracks

-earth-wind-and-fire-thats-the-way-of-the-world. P. Bailey, *Shining Star*, p. 139.

15  P. Bailey, *Shining Star*, p. 122. M. White, *My Life*, p. 125. V. White, personal communication, 2021.

16  Gordon E. Thompson. (2016). *Black Music, Black Poetry: Blues and Jazz's Impact on African American Versification*. New York: Routledge, p. 80.

17  Rickey Vincent. (1996). *Funk: The Music, the People, and the Rhythm of the One*. New York: St. Martin's Griffin, p. 69.

18  Vincent's comprehensive analysis of funk music mischaracterizes EWF a funk band.

19  Ron Wynn. (1999). "A Felicidade (Celebration)." CD Notes on 1999 re-release of *All 'N All*.

20  *Shining Stars: The Official Story of Earth, Wind & Fire.*

21  P. Bailey, *Shining Star*, p. 108.

22  O. Jordan, "5 Funk Guitarists."

23  Scott Freiman. (March 4, 2016). "What Made 'Shining Star' Burn So Bright?" *Culture Sonar*. Accessed April 5, 2020. https://www.culturesonar.com/what-made-shining-star-burn-so-bright/.

24  In the context of this song, vamp refers to the short sequence of chords that gets repeated for an extended period: "Shining star for you to see what your life can truly be."

25  Robyn Flans. (December 1, 2004). "Classic Tracks: Earth, Wind & Fire's 'Shining Star.'" *Mix*. Accessed May 15, 2021. https://web.archive.org/web/20091110222902/ http://mixonline.com/mag/audio earth wind fires/.

26  R. Flans, "Classic Tracks."

27  V. White, Personal Communication.

## Chapter 6

1   A. Dozer. (2020). *The Velvet Rope*. New York: Bloomsbury, pp. 12–13. Perhaps it is fitting the two artists to effectively use interludes on albums announced their collaboration (along with Jimmy Jam and Terry Lewis) on Jackson's next album, to be released in 2022.

2   "The 50 Greatest Interludes of All Time: Staff Picks." *Billboard*. March 9, 2018. Accessed September 30, 2021. https://www.billboard.com/articles/columns/pop/8235597/greatest-interludes-of-all-time-top-50-list/.

3   Robert Christgau. (2020). "That's the Way of the World." *Consumer Guide Album*. Accessed May 12, 2020. https://www.robertchristgau.com/get_artist.php?id=399.

4   Mosi Reeves, Jason Heller, et al. (February 5, 2016). "Earth, Wind & Fire: 12 Essential Songs." *Rolling Stone*. Accessed June 20, 2021. https://www.rollingstone.com/music/music-lists/earth-wind-fire-12-essential-songs-26670/lets-groove-1981-28085/.

5   Dan Charnas. (2020). "The Song That Never Ends: Why Earth, Wind & Fire's 'September' Sustains." Accessed June 12, 2020. https://www.rollingstone.com/music/albumreviews/earth-wind-fire-19710624.

6   One interview with Ramsey Lewis incorrectly identified Al McKay as the guitarist White brought to Chicago. Ironically, White confirmed it was Johnny Graham who joined him in Chicago, although when the recording session was not going well, he said he felt he needed Al McKay. J. L. Richardson. "Ramsey Lewis: The History Makers." The History Makers Digital Archive. Session 2, tape 5, story 3. M. White, *My Life*, p. 160.

## Chapter 7

1 M. White, *My Life*, p. 175.

2 V. White, personal communication, 2021.

3 William Banfield, Personal Communication, May 2020.

4 One example is George Chesterton's description of the song as about as good as it gets. (April 2, 2012). "Old Music: Earth, Wind & Fire—That's the Way of the World." *The Guardian.* Accessed July 9, 2021. https://www.theguardian.com/music/musicblog/2012/apr/02/earth-wind-fire-way-world.

5 Among the alternative readings of this song is a critique of the music industry.

6 Ross Boissoneau. (2021). "Bluey of Incognito: The Albums That Shaped My Career." Accessed July 25, 2021. https://somethingelsereviews.com/2021/07/23/bluey-incognito-marvin-gaye-stevie-wonder/.

## Epilogue

1 V. White, personal communication, 2021.

2 Robert Palmer. (October 21, 1979). "How Funk Grew Up". *New York Times.* Accessed August 28, 2021. https://www.nytimes.com/1979/10/21/archives/how-funk-grew-up.html. Palmer's review of *I Am* situates EWF's "exceptional musicianship" in a broader discussion of funk and critique of essentialist notions of Black authenticity.

3 Geoffrey Himes. (February 9, 2016). "Maurice White: The Flame Within Earth, Wind & Fire." *Paste Magazine.* Accessed

August 28, 2021. https://www.pastemagazine.com/music/ earth-wind-fire/maurice-white/. Himes offsets his criticism of White's lyrics by giving him credit for introducing third-world elements into American popular music long before it became a trend.

4   Barack Obama. (2020). *A Promised Land.* New York: Crown, p. 287.

# Also Available in the Series

# ALSO AVAILABLE IN THE SERIES